Setterly Yours

A Photographic Introduction
to
The English Setter

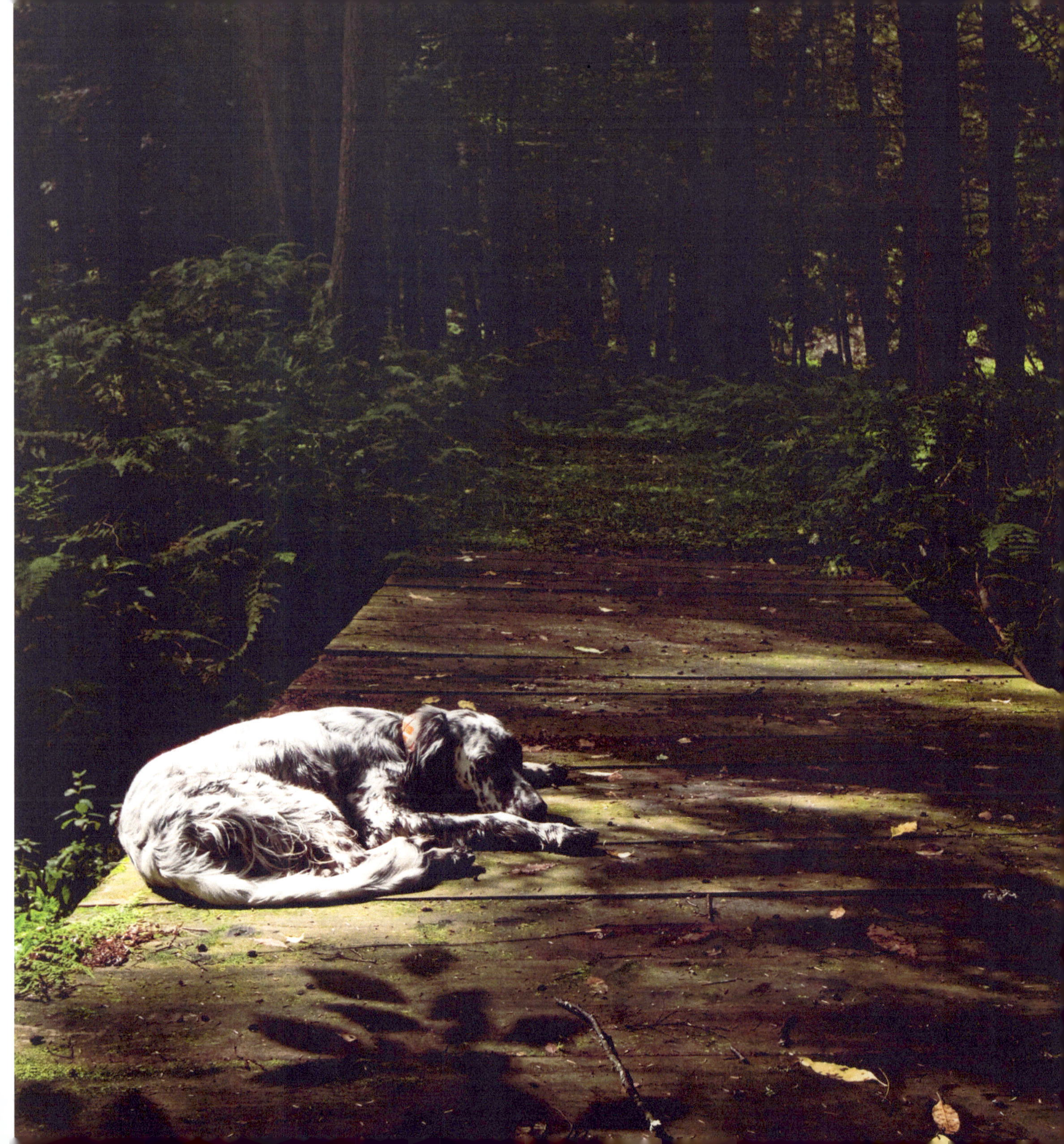

DANICA BARREAU

Setterly Yours

A Photographic Introduction
to
The English Setter

Second Edition

for Carter, my inspiration

Setterly Yours
A Photographic Introduction to The English Setter
Second Edition

www.pouka.com

First Edition published in 2009

For more information address: info@pouka.com

ISBN - 978-0-9981746-0-0 - Hardback
ISBN - 978-0-9981746-1-7 - Paperback

Printed in the United States of America
Book design by Pouka, LLC

Contents

Introduction

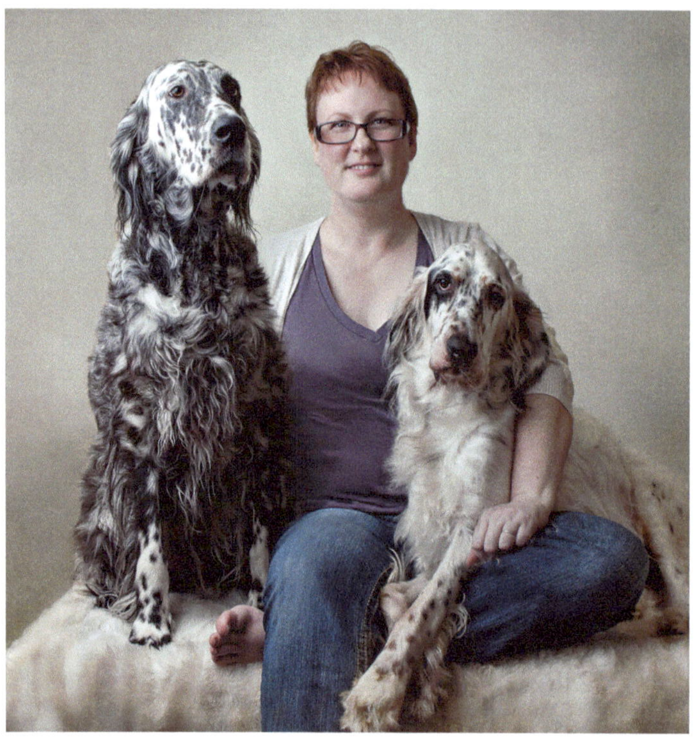

I adopted my first English Setter in 2005. My family had always had gun dogs; at the time we had two Golden Retrievers and I'd recently lost my beloved Flat Coated Retriever to cancer. I'd admired the gracefulness and beauty of English Setters from afar so when I decided to adopt one, I tried doing breed research beforehand. But I found most of the breed specific information dealt with lists of facts, breed history, and pictures of show dogs, none of which really prepared me for the enthusiasm of a young field-type Setter.

The first few years with Carter, a deaf blue belton Llewellin, were an adventure. He was incredibly active, very smart, constantly getting into trouble, and the light of my life. He taught me so much about canine behavior, dog training, veterinary issues, bird dog instincts, and patience. Lots and lots of patience. Social media became a "thing" and Carter was a minor celebrity in the English Setter rescue world due to both his antics and his good looks. I became heavily involved in rescue and fostered over twenty English Setters - I was head-over-heels in love with the breed. In 2009 I wrote, compiled, and published the first edition of "Setterly Yours", hoping to provide a different type of information about English Setters to prospective families.

I lost Carter to cancer in the spring of 2013, shortly after his 8th birthday and just three months after I brought home my second English Setter, Sparrow. In 2014, another deaf English Setter, Finch, joined our family. These stunning dogs have introduced me to so many fantastic new people, taken me on adventures across the country, and have inspired me to grow my photography into a business. I decided a second expanded edition of "Setterly Yours" was required with more details about this amazing breed and, of course, many more photographs!

I hope you enjoy this book and that it provides a window into the magnificent world of English Setters!

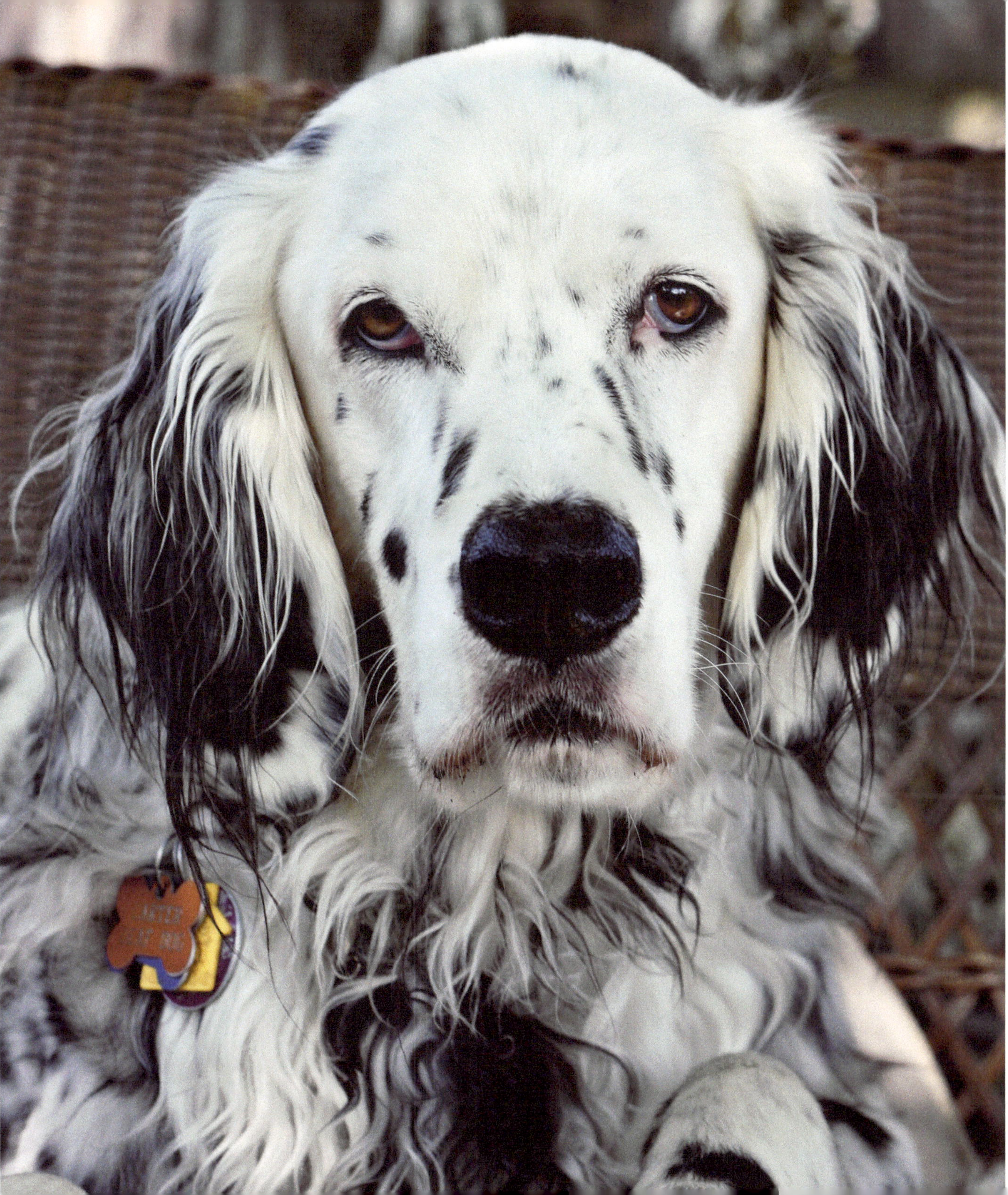

Setterly Yours

A Photographic Introduction
to
The English Setter

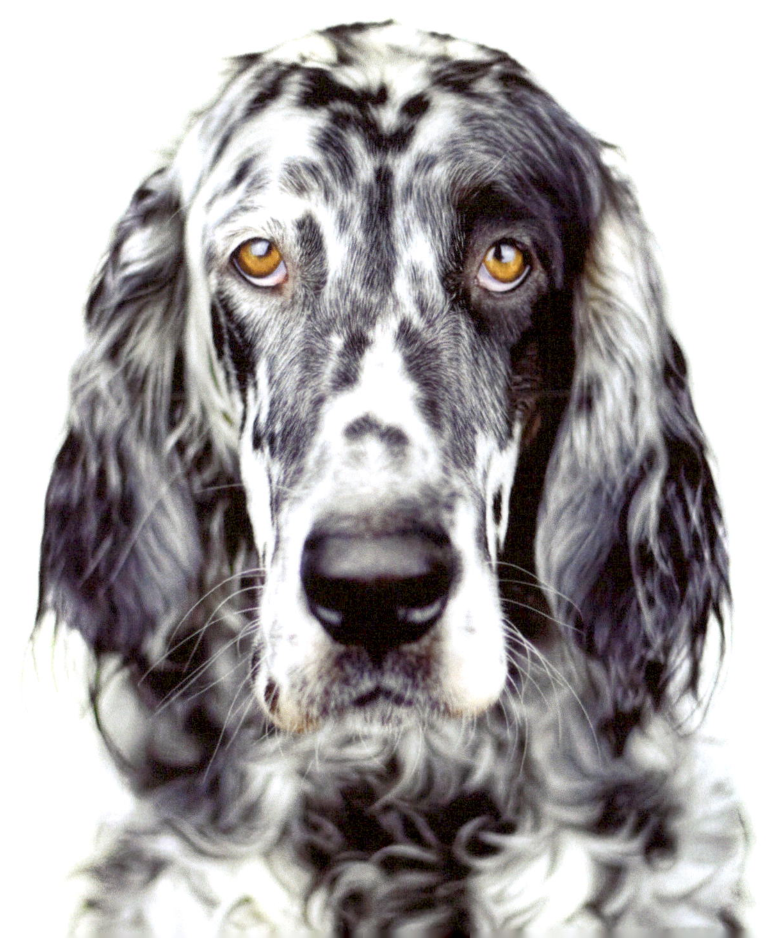

What is a Setter?

Setters are bird hunting dogs that can trace their history in Europe back to the 14th century. They were used to find game birds such as quail, grouse, partridge, pheasants, and any other bird that would try to hide by remaining still rather than flying off at the first sign of danger. The dogs would range out in front of hunters and track the scent of the birds with their fabulous noses. Once they were close they would crouch down, or "set", and use their motionless bodies to indicate to the hunters exactly where the birds were hiding. Their low-to-the-ground profile would keep them from being entangled in the nets the hunters used to catch the birds. That crouch is why they were named "setters".

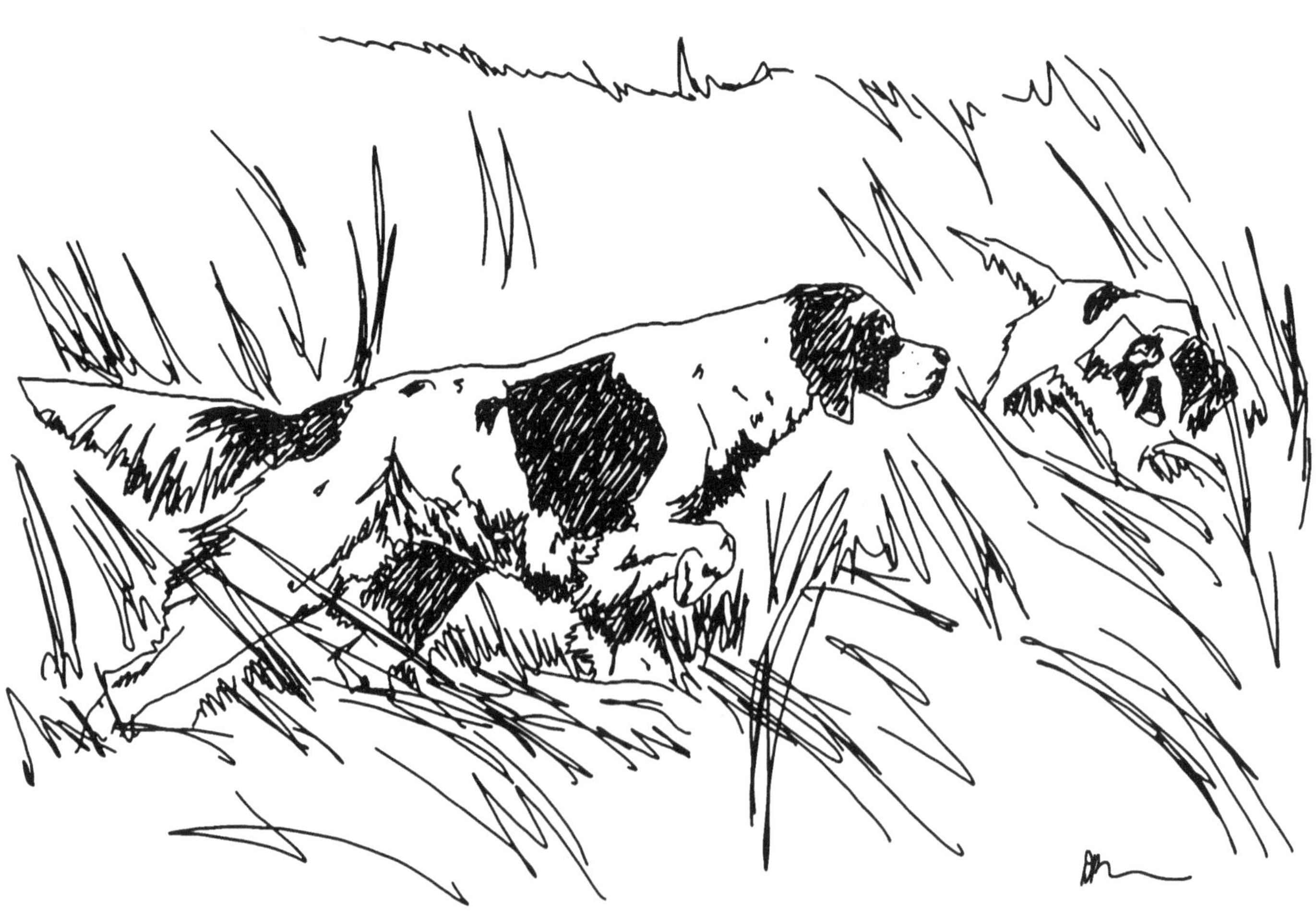

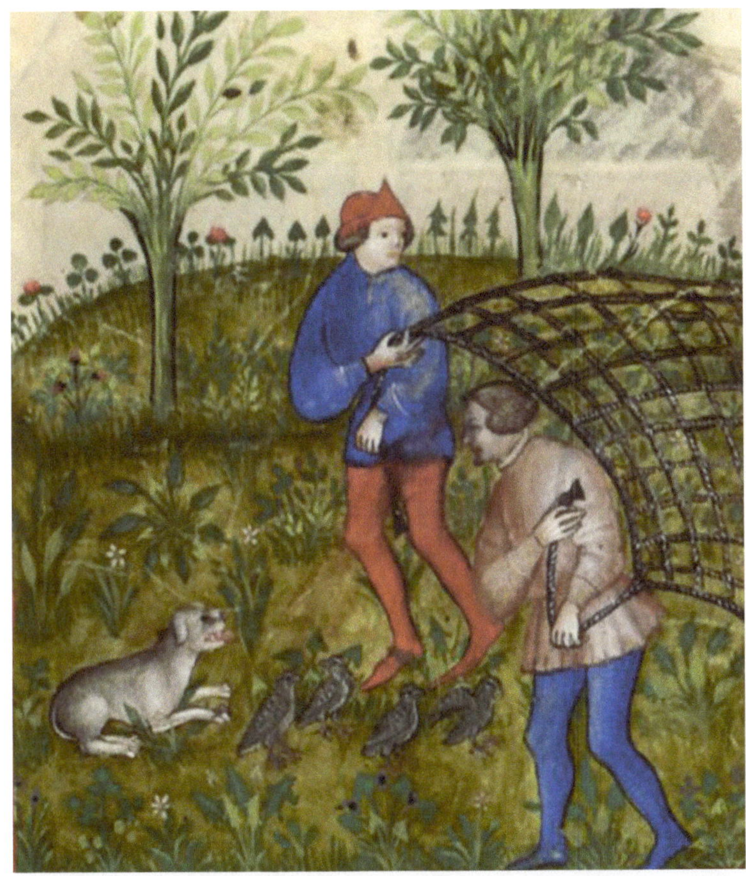

The image on the left is from a page in a 1390 manuscript called "Tacuinum Sanitatis" and shows a dog "setting" partridges while the hunters use a net. Generations of breeding for both form and function distilled the most desirable traits to develop today's Setters, capable of finding and retrieving upland game birds.

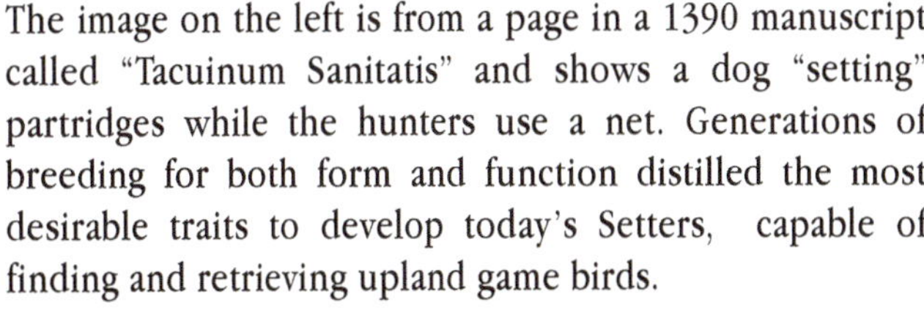

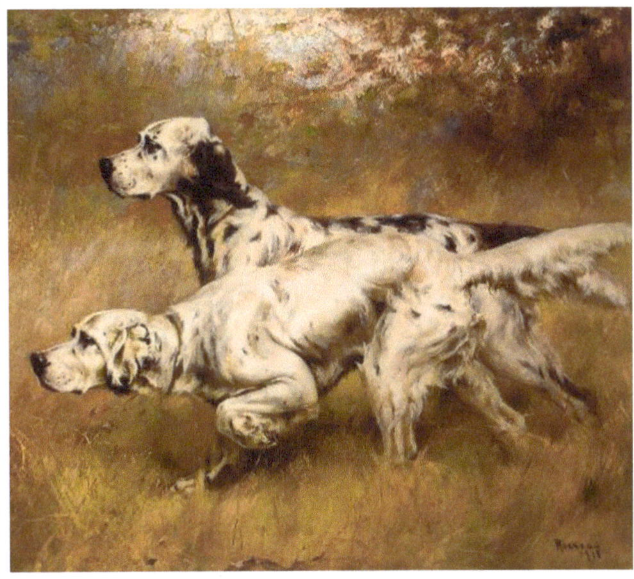

The image above is a Percival Rousseau painting from 1918 and shows how the English Setter developed into its own distinct breed over 500 years.

Since nets have been replaced by guns, the need for setters to set so close to the ground has disappeared. The modern setter is taller than its ancestors and, although some setters still retain the instinct to drop down into a set, most will freeze in mid-stride to point out a bird's hiding spot. Tail position, body size, and the amount of coat color varies wildly depending on the terrain in which the dogs are being worked. A darker colored dog might be more desireable in areas with a lot of snow. A "12 o'clock tail" might more useful for hunters working in heavy tall grass rather than a perpendicular tail. The active use of the English Setter as a hunting dog world-wide is why there is such a range of looks within a single breed.

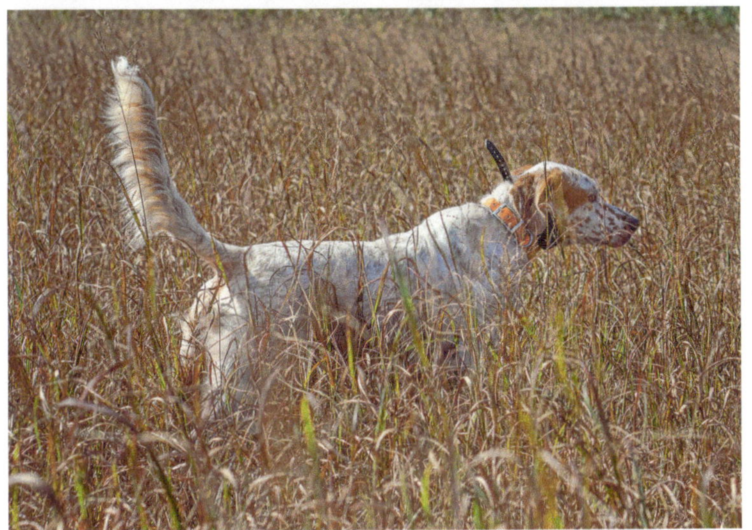

The English Setter is also an able retrieving dog, bringing the downed birds back to the hunter.

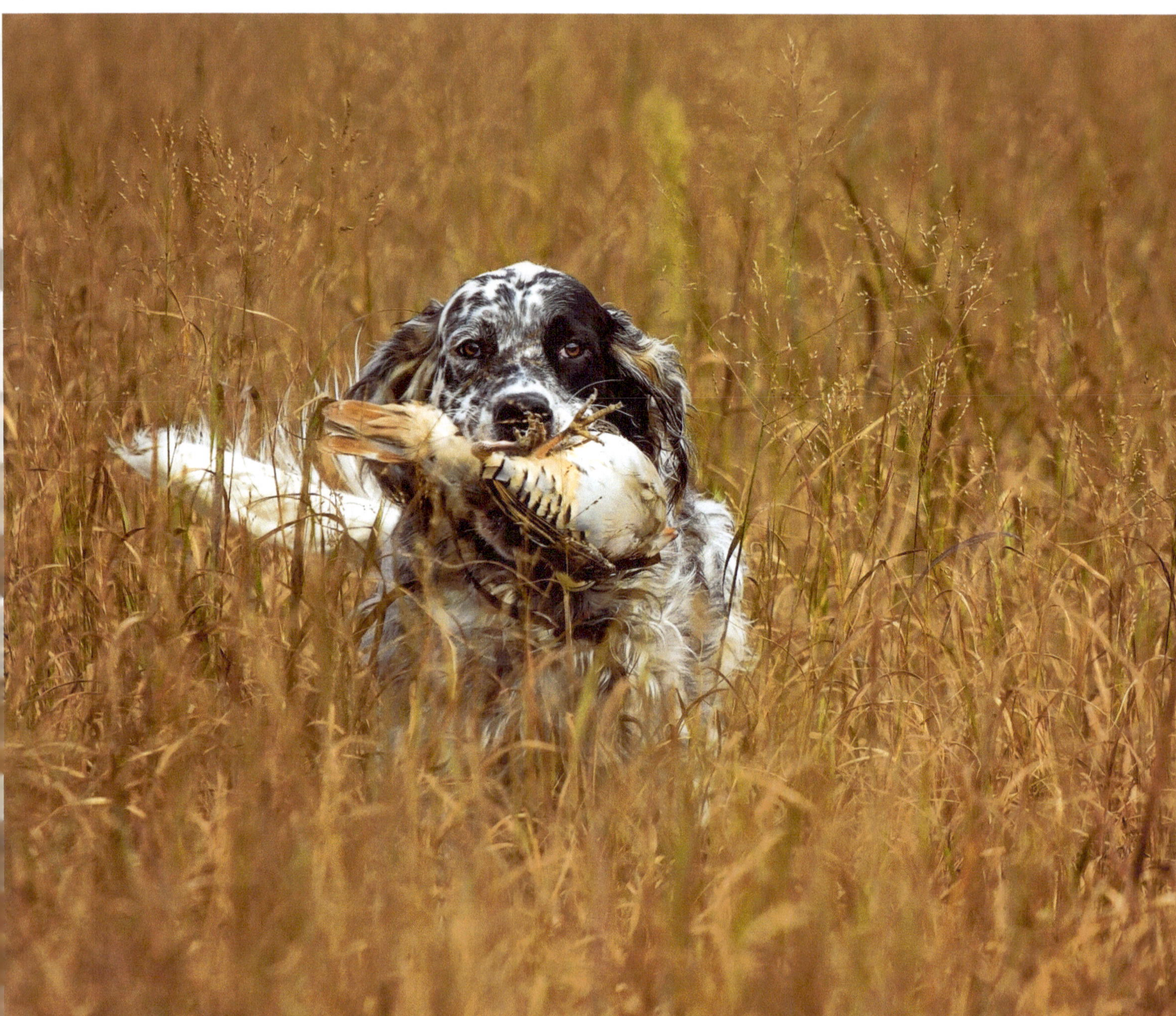

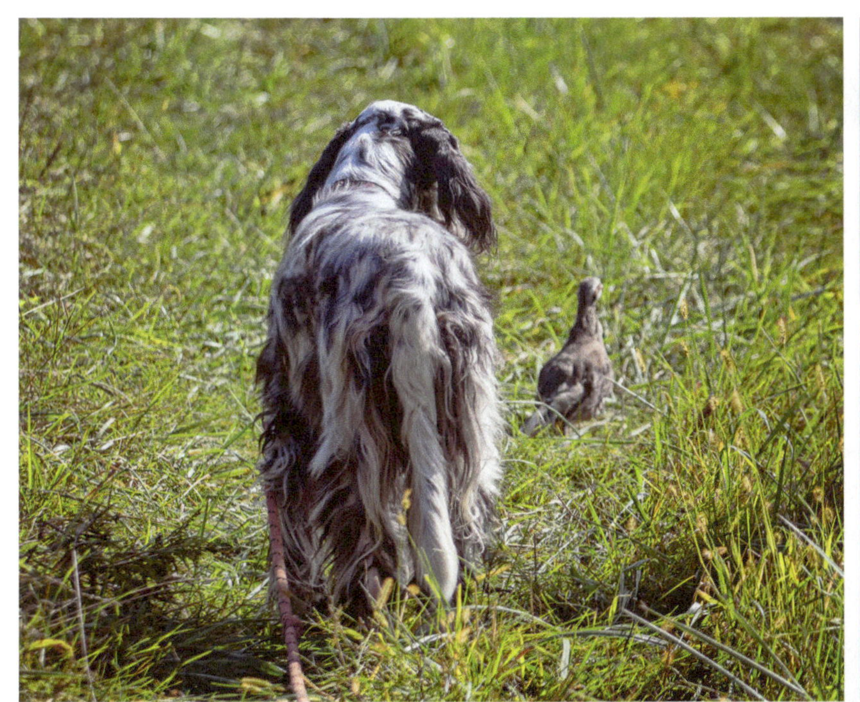

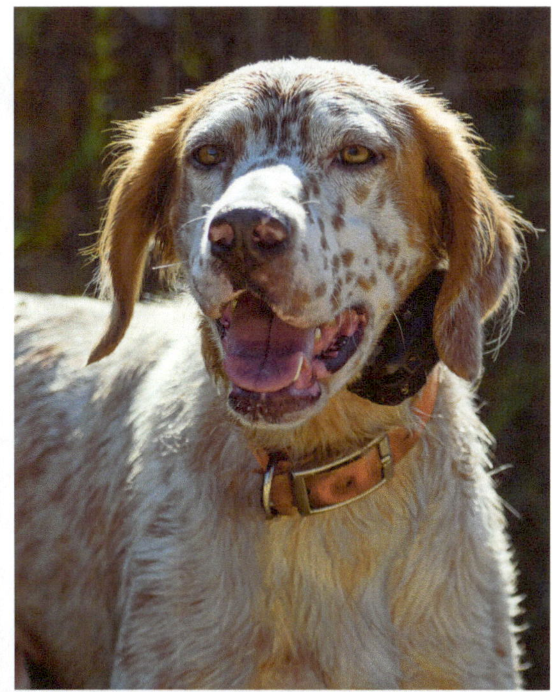

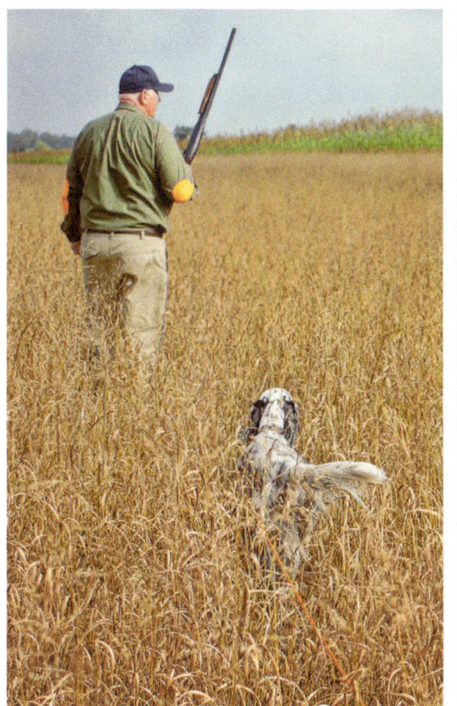

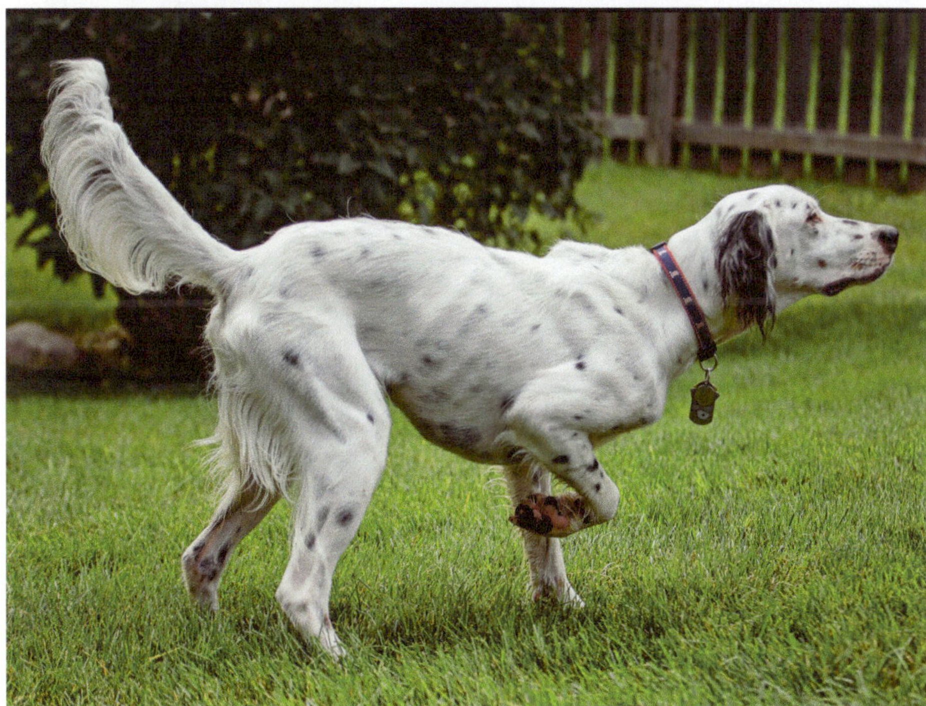

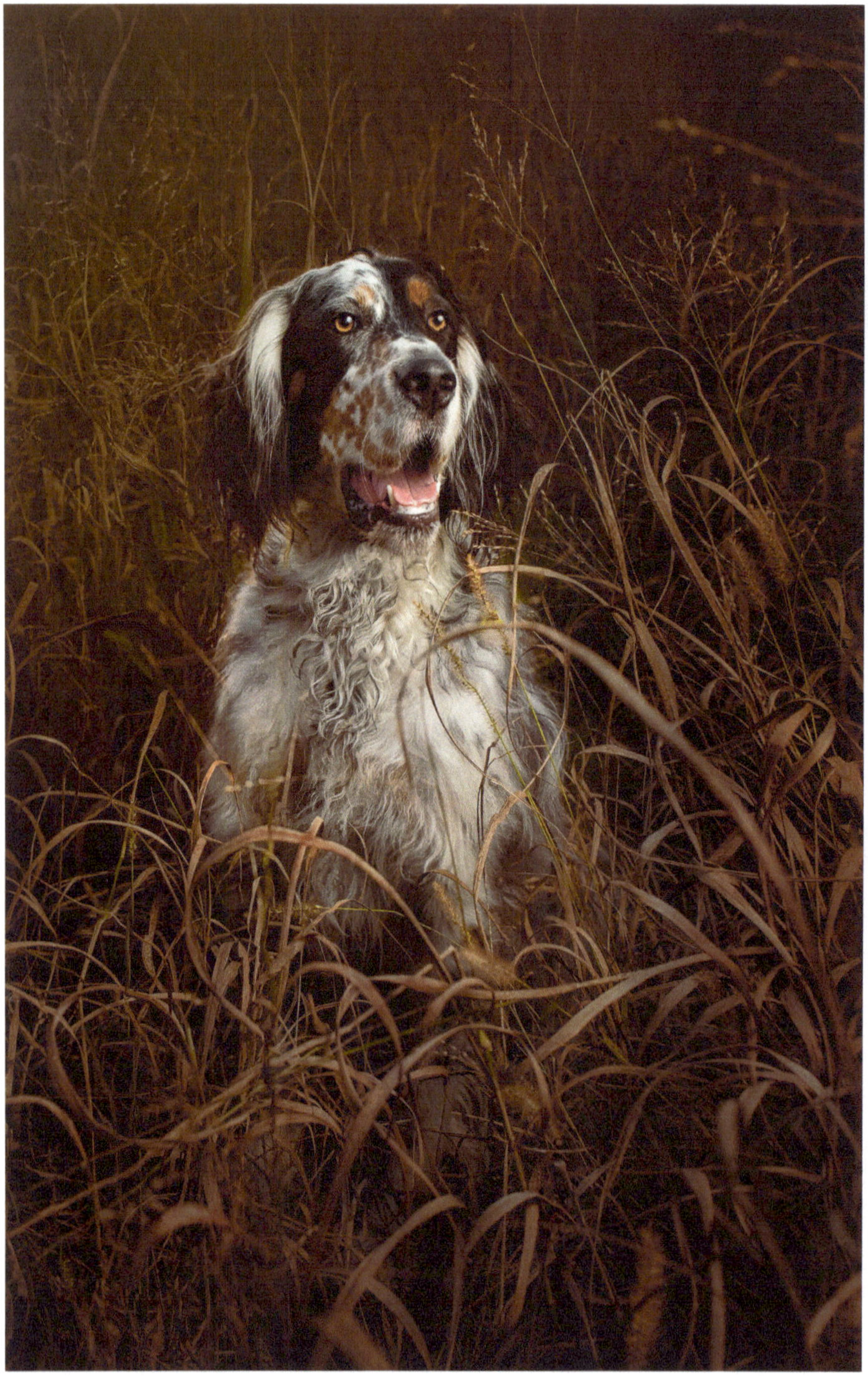

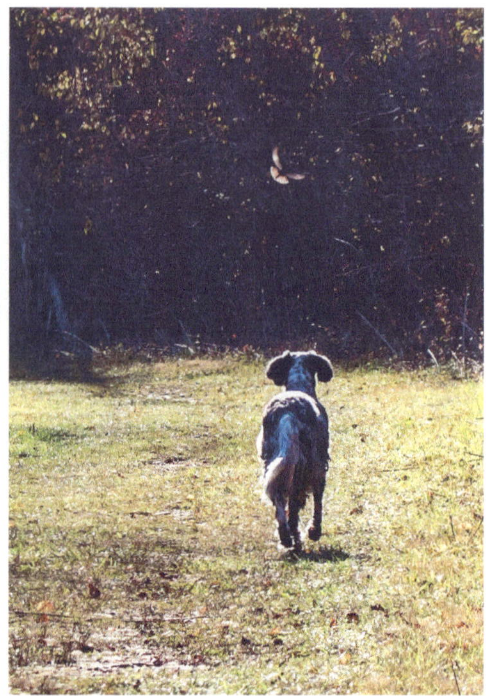

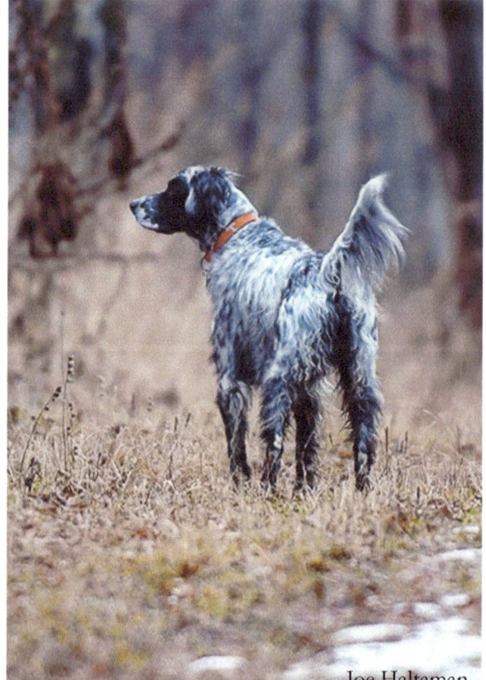

Joe Haltaman

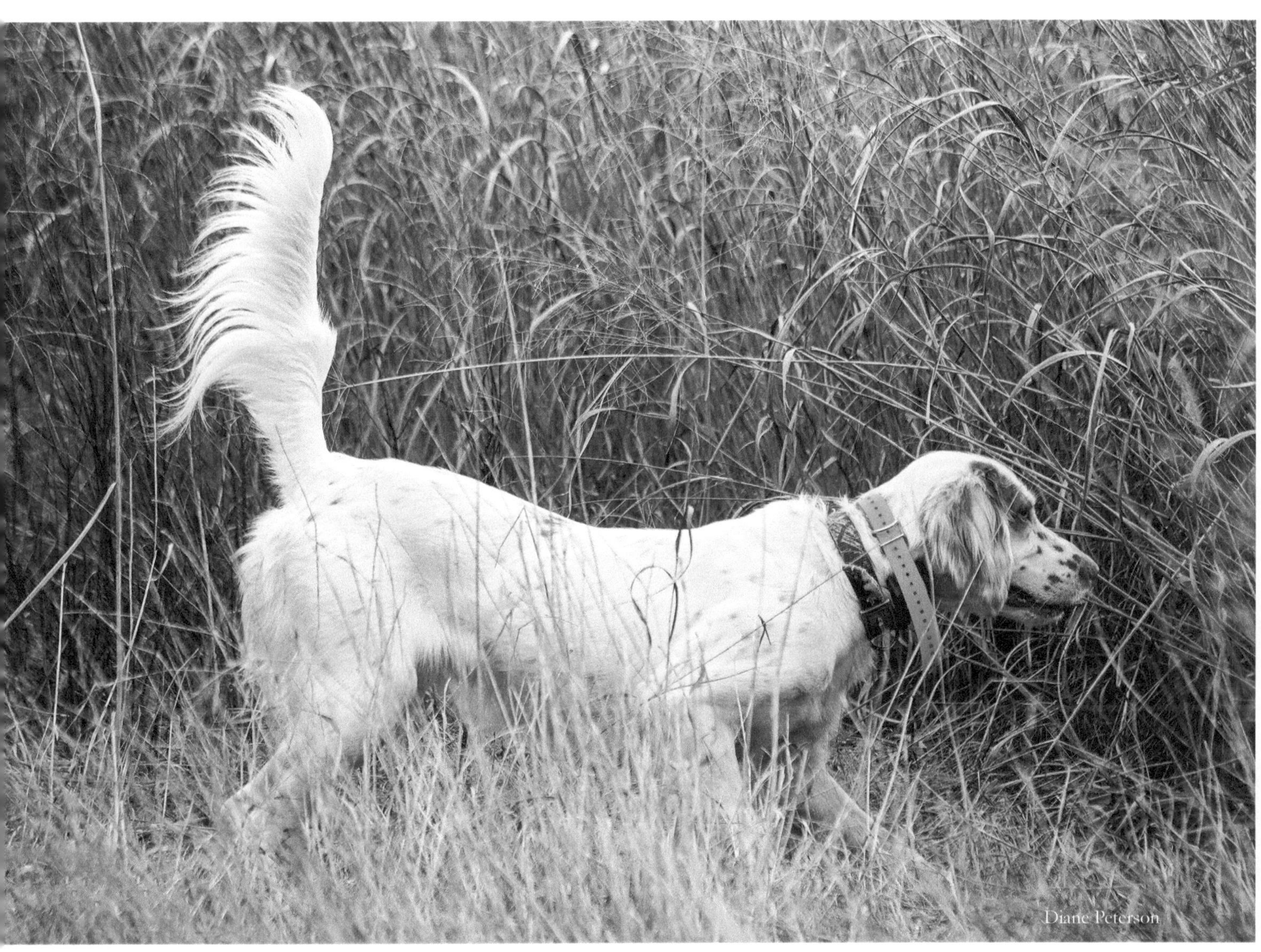
Diane Peterson

Today, there are four different types of Setters: The Irish, Gordon, Irish Red and White, and English. Setters were a single breed until people started to breed them for different hunting characteristics as well as looks. Now, all the Setter breeds look and often behave differently from each other while still retaining the instinct to set.

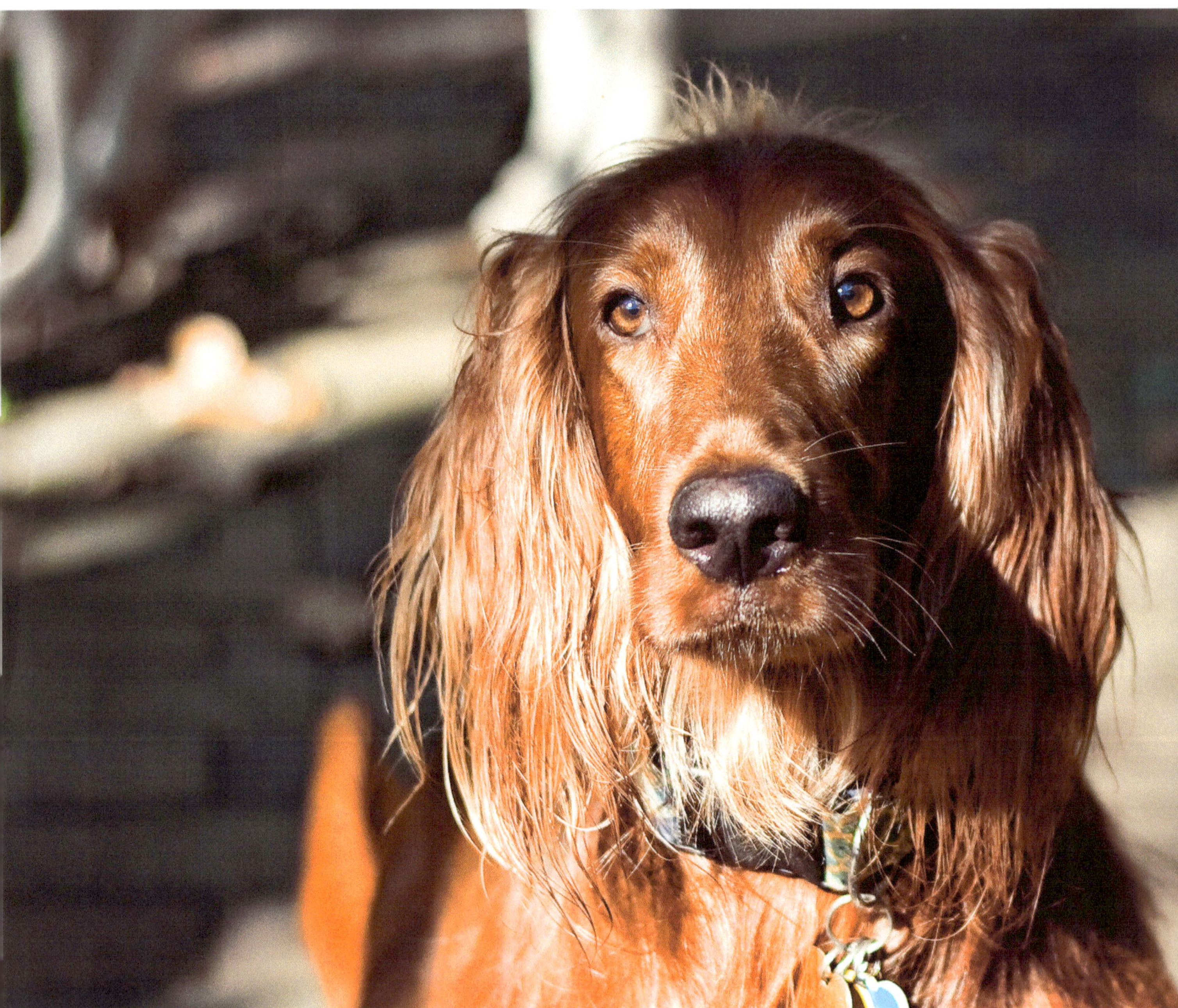

The Irish Setter

The Irish Setter rightly deserves its reputation as a mischievous clown. Described as a fun-loving breed, the Irish have an outgoing personality that pairs well with their striking dark red coats. The Irish, like the English, have both field and show lines. Both make good pets, though the field lines are usually smaller with shorter coats. Field line Irish Setters registered with the Field Dog Stud Book, an alternative to the AKC, are sometimes called "Red Setters".

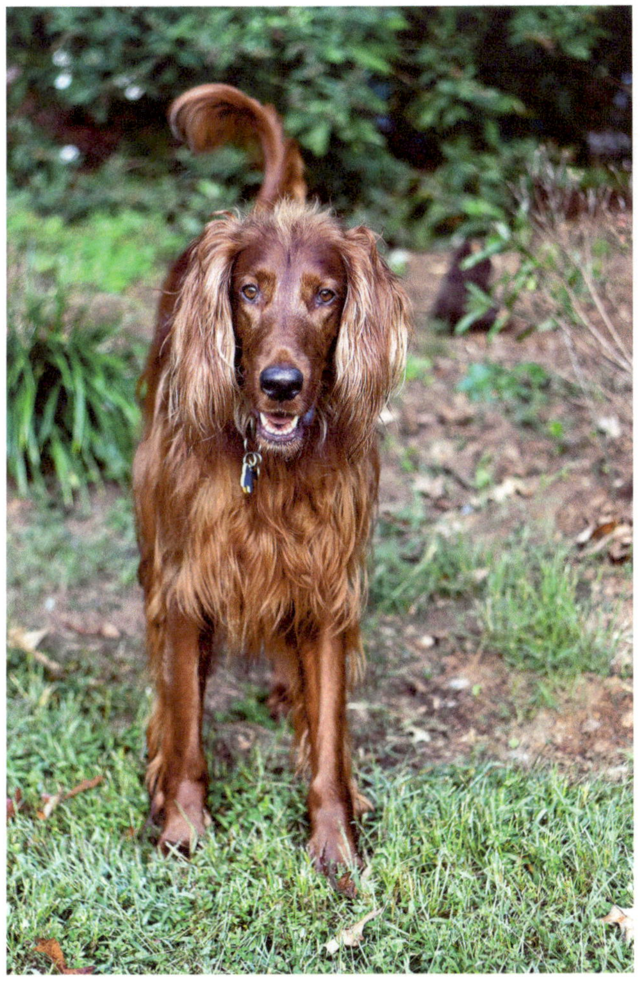

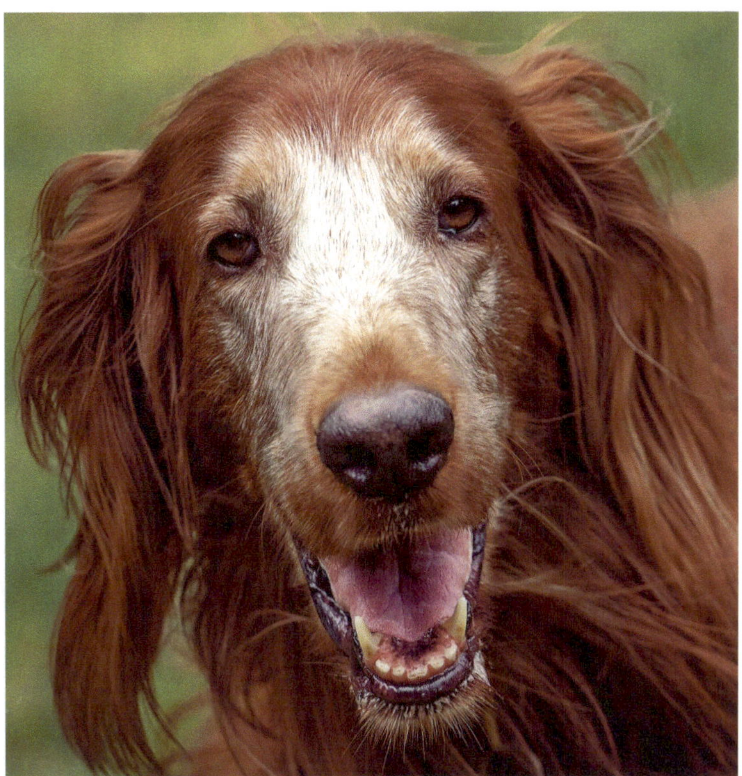

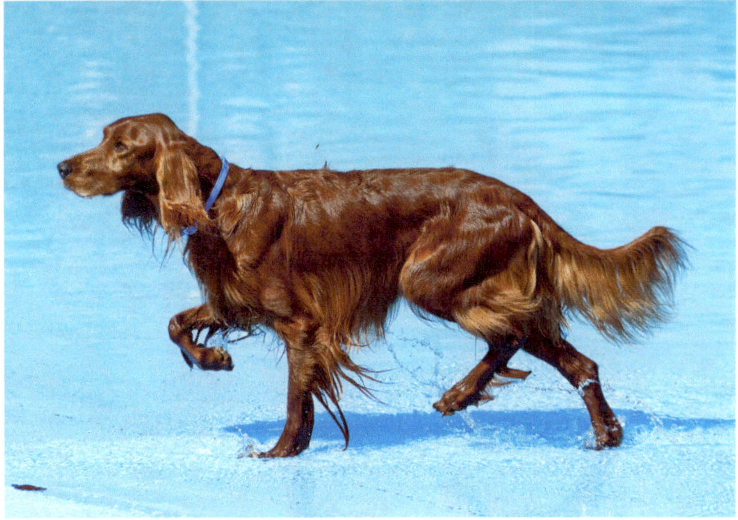

The Gordon Setter

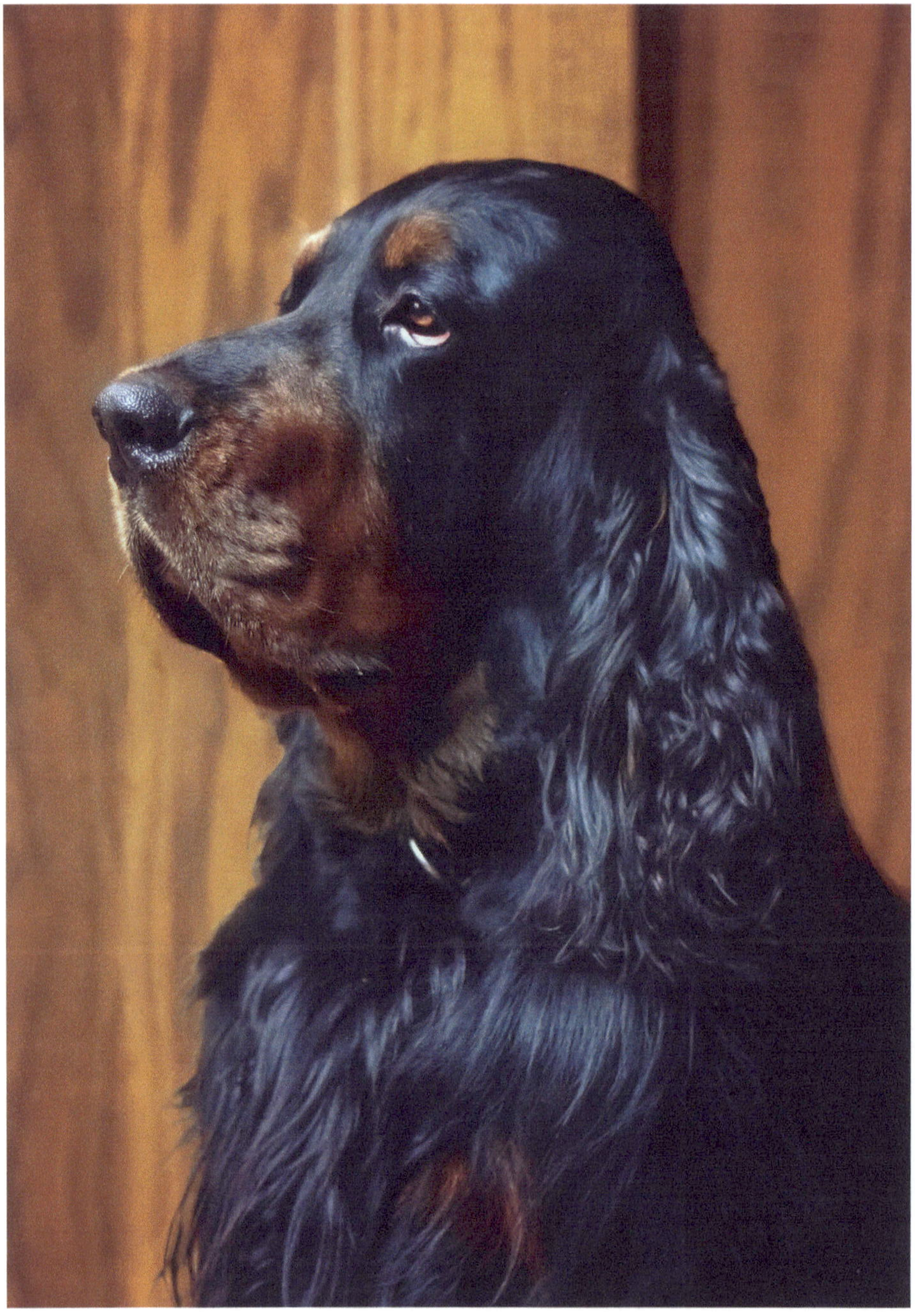

The black and tan Gordon Setters are the heaviest of the Setters and hail from Scotland. Their distinctive coat allows them to be found easily in light fields and early snow and they are prized as an excellent one-man shooting dog. They are alert and confident and, like all Setters, devoted to their families.

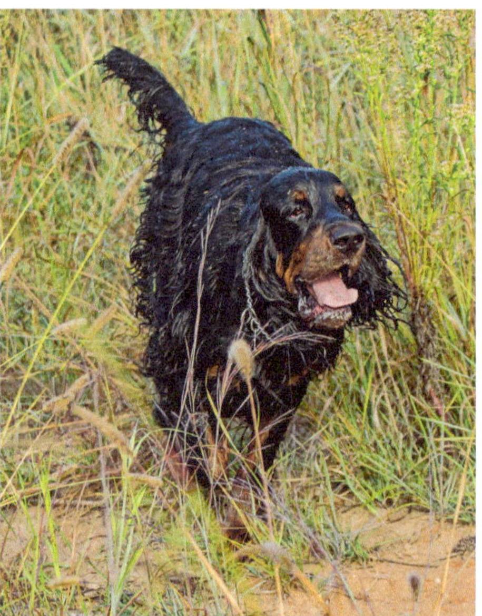

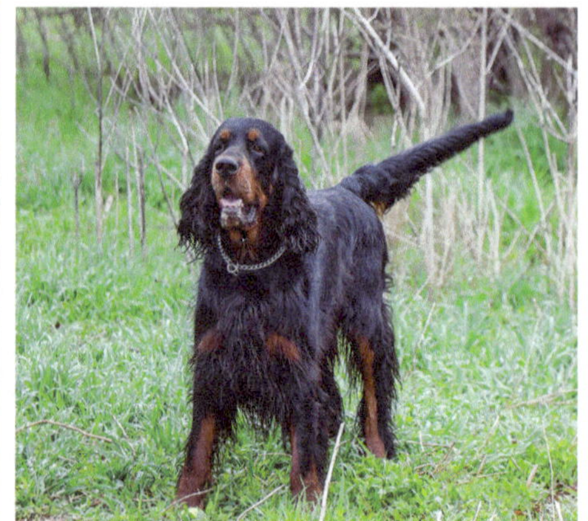

The original Irish Setter was described as red and white but, over the years, all red dogs were preferred in the show ring. The red and white colored Irish Setter almost completely disappeared until a concerted effort was made to revive the color in the 1970's and they were registered with the AKC as their own distinct breed, the Irish Red and White Setter, in 2009. Their kind and friendly attitudes make them great family dogs.

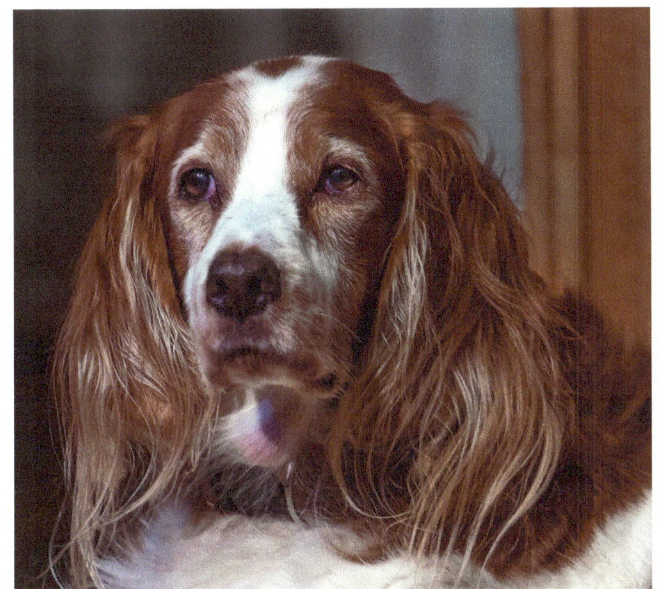

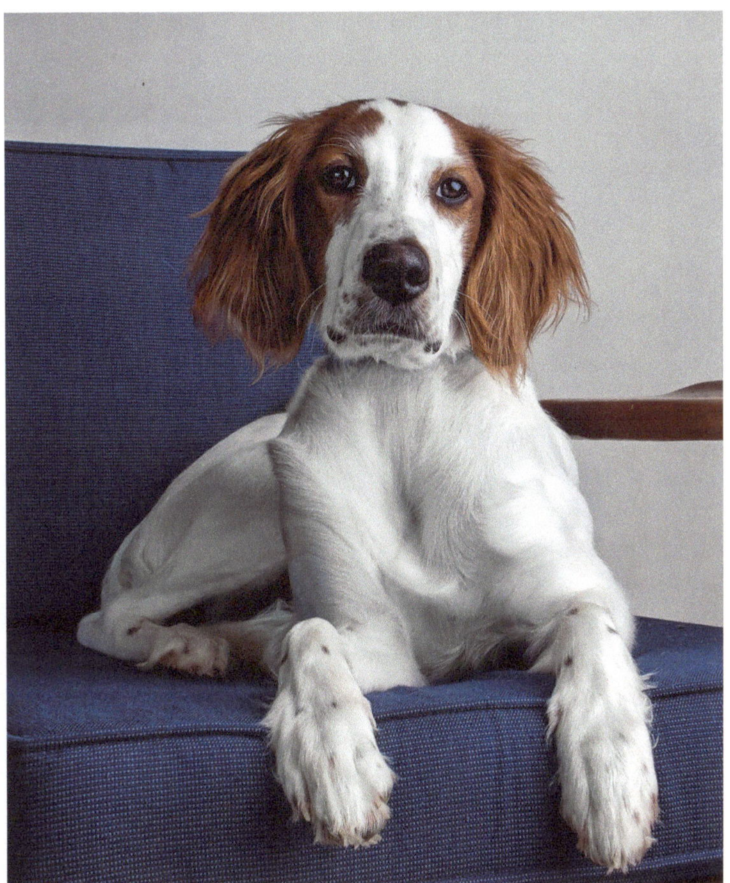

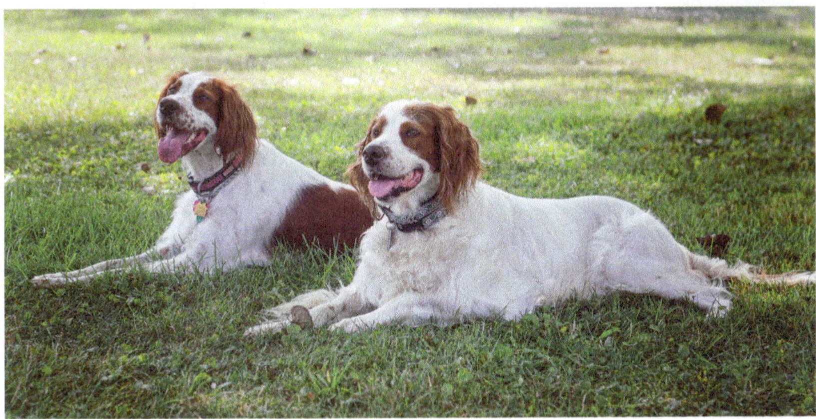

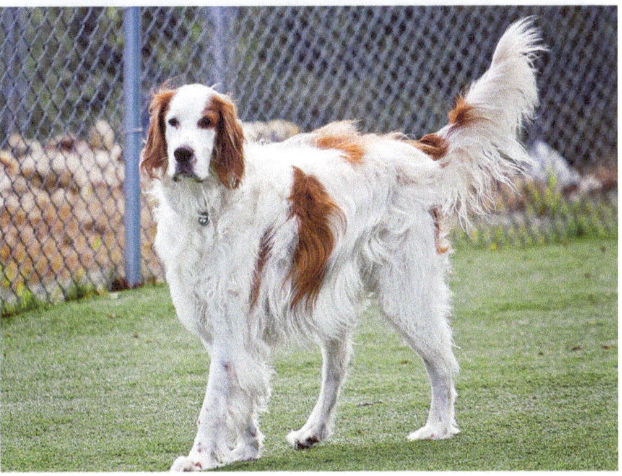

The English Setter

Even within the individual Setter breeds there is a lot of variety. English Setters come in many different colors, shapes, and sizes. The English Setters you see on TV during the dog shows may look very different from the dogs you see hunting in the field. There is no "right" or "wrong" type. Every English Setter is an enthusiastic bird dog with a quirky personality, regardless of their coat, color, or size.

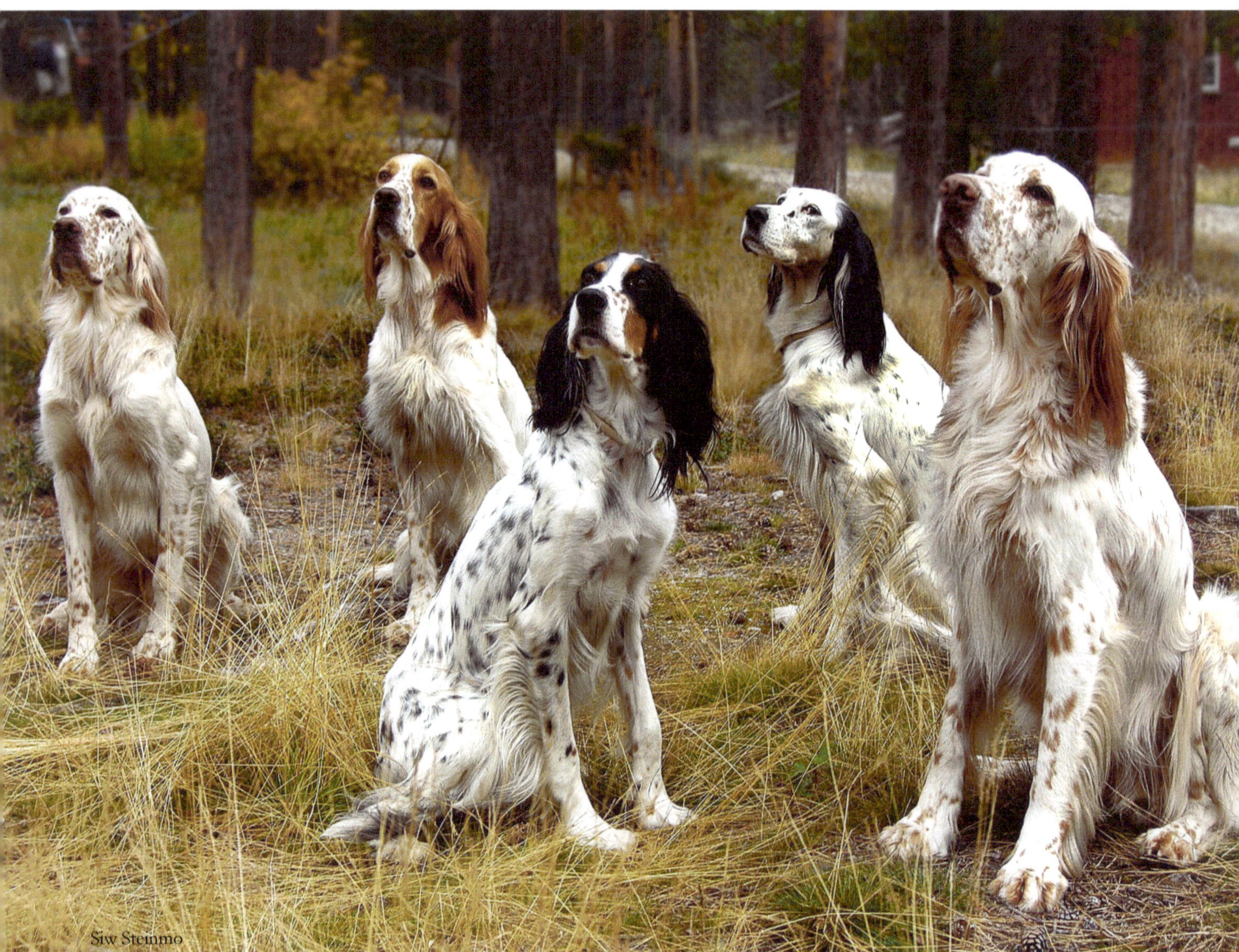

Today there are arguably four English setter types in the United States - bench, Llewellin, field, and Ryman.

The dogs you see at the American Kennel Club (AKC) dog shows today are described as "Bench" Setters. Some all-breed shows require dogs to stay in an assigned "benching area" for the duration of the show, so that the public can easily view the dogs and talk to the breeders, owners, and handlers. The term eventually grew to mean an English Setter that was bred from AKC registered show lines. These dogs have bigger heads, with longer flews, and very long coats. In the opinion of some, the hunting ability of bench dogs was compromised by the focus on their looks so there has been a push to create a "dual dog" bench Setter, which can both hunt and show.

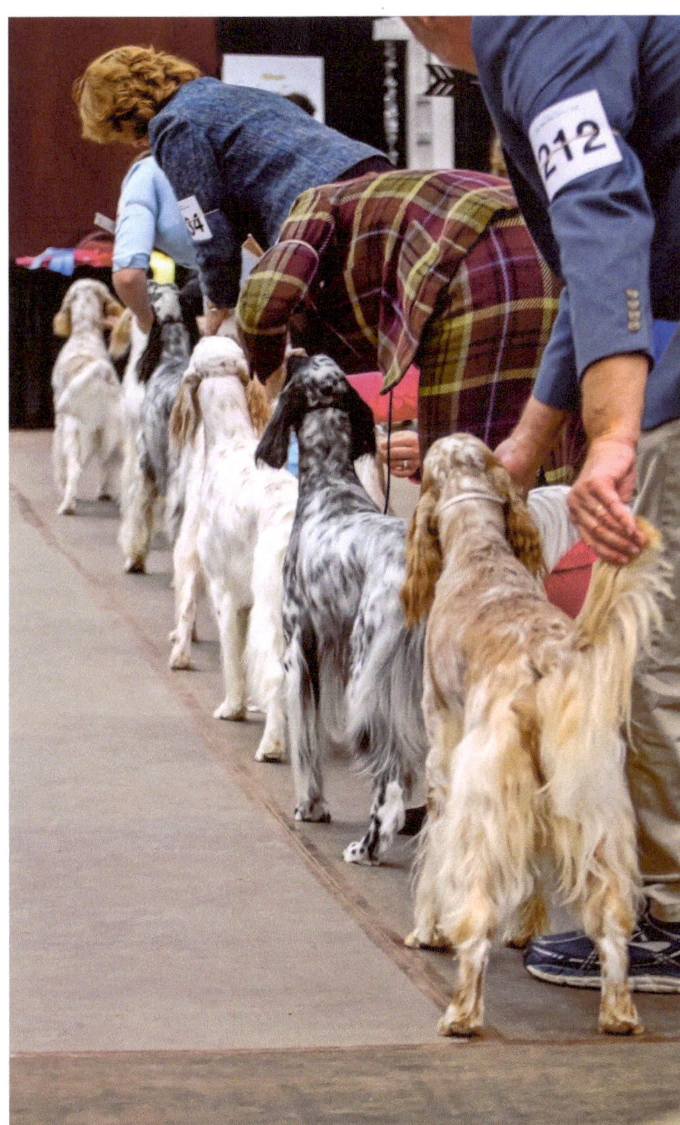

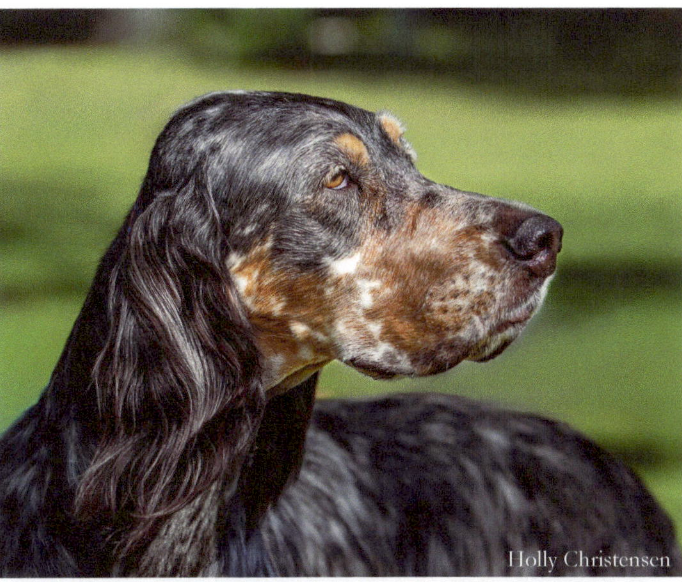
Holly Christensen

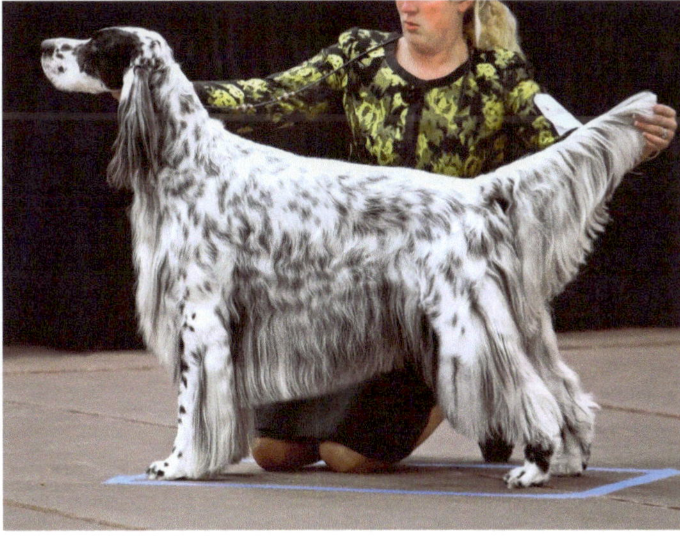

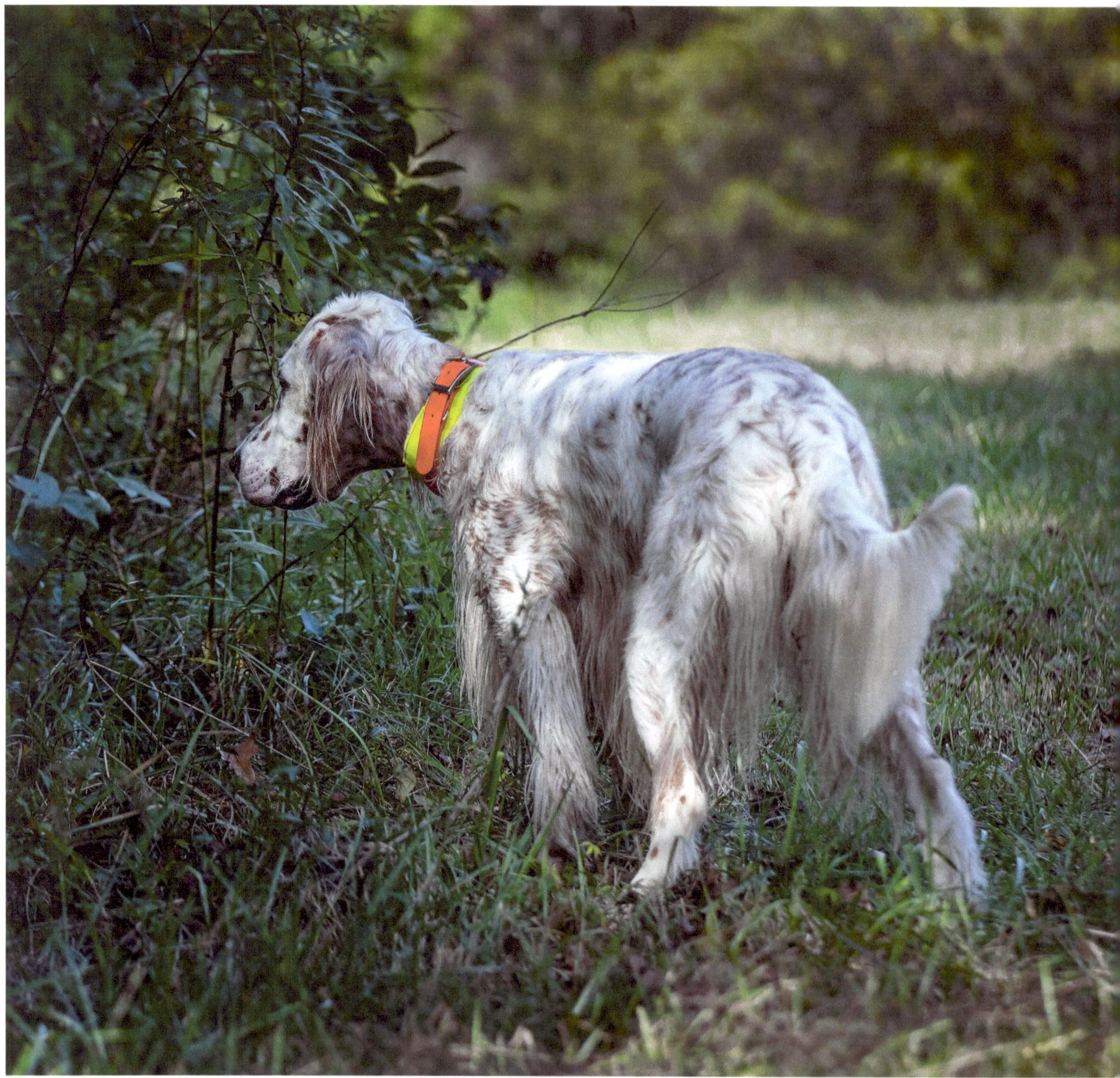

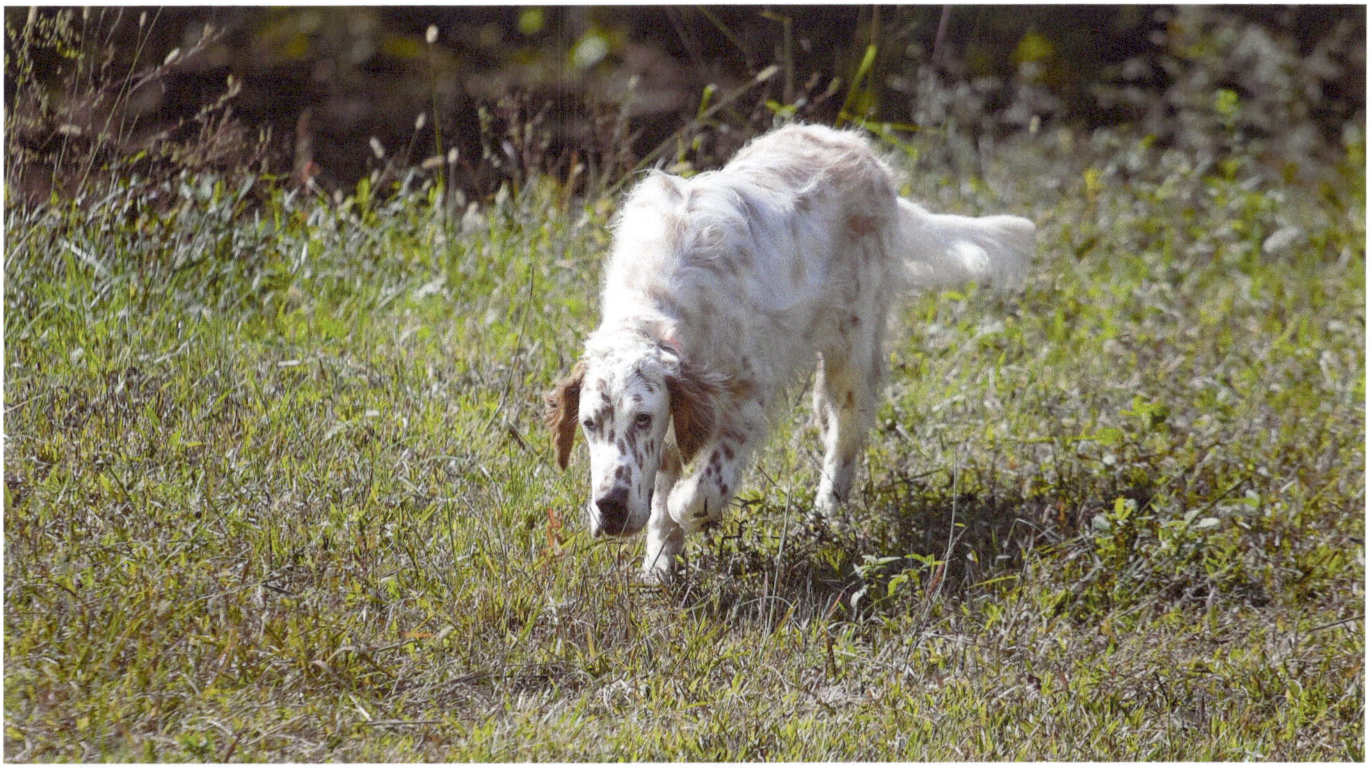

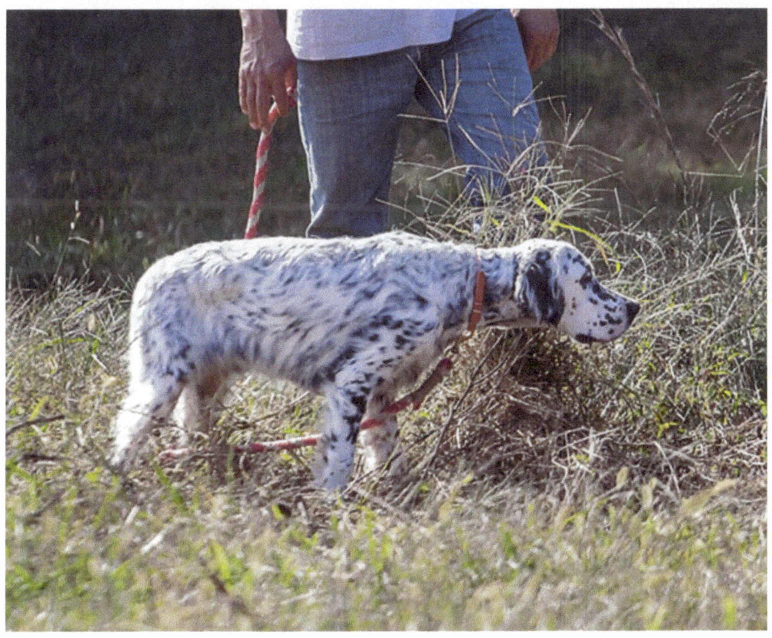
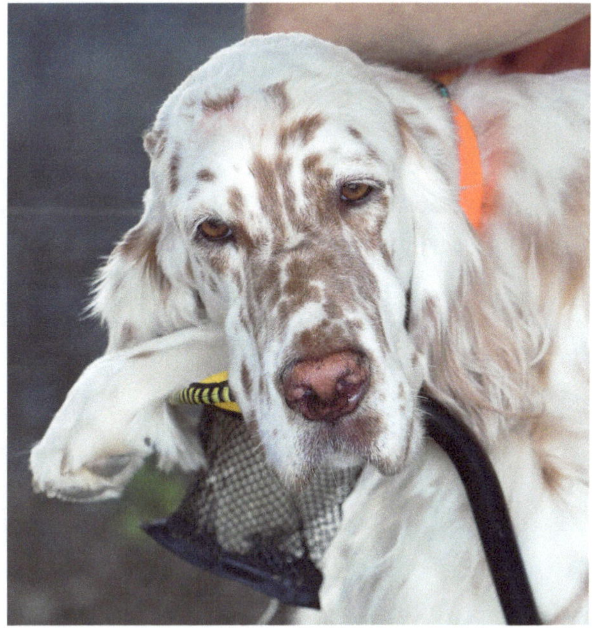

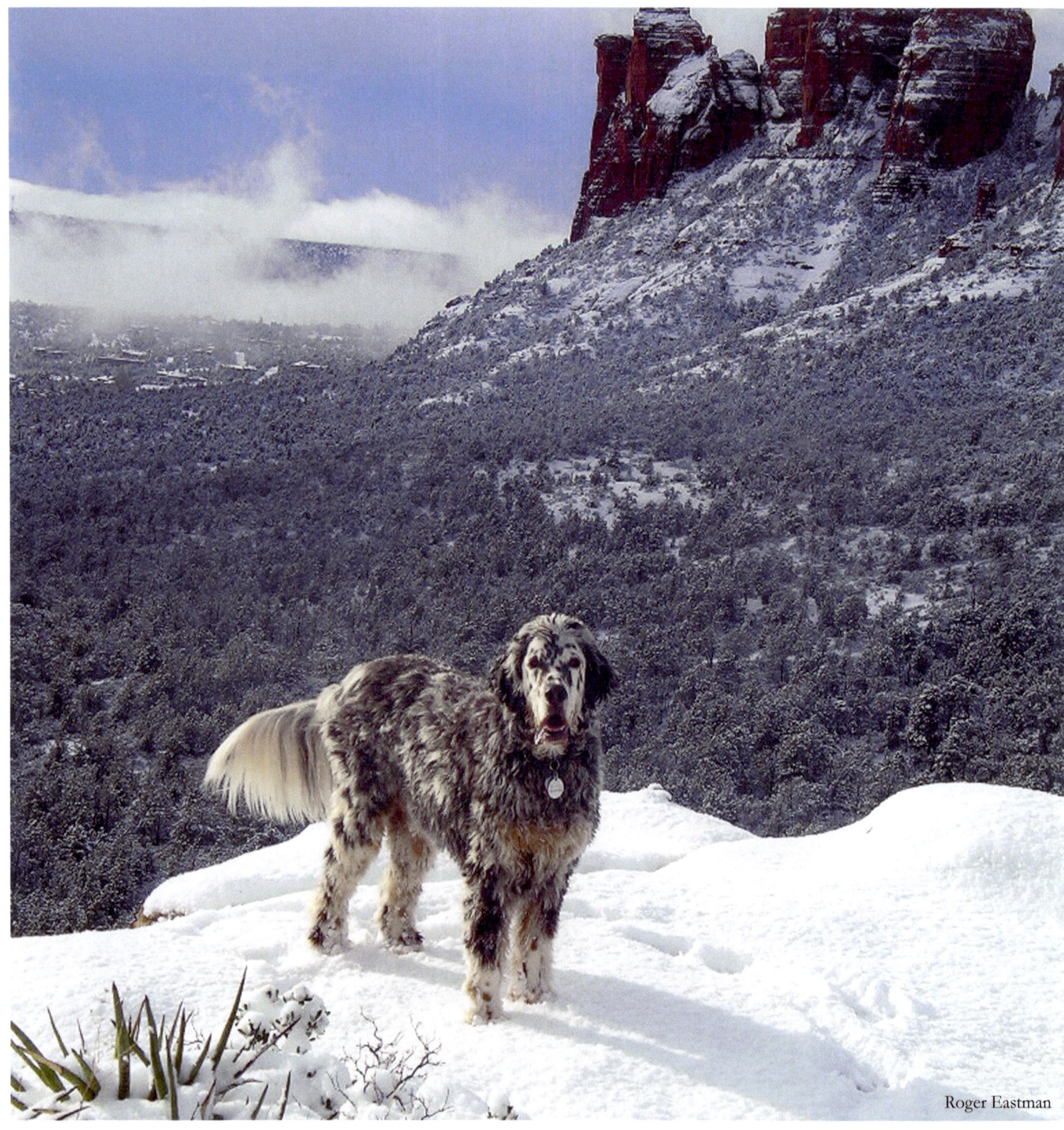

Roger Eastman

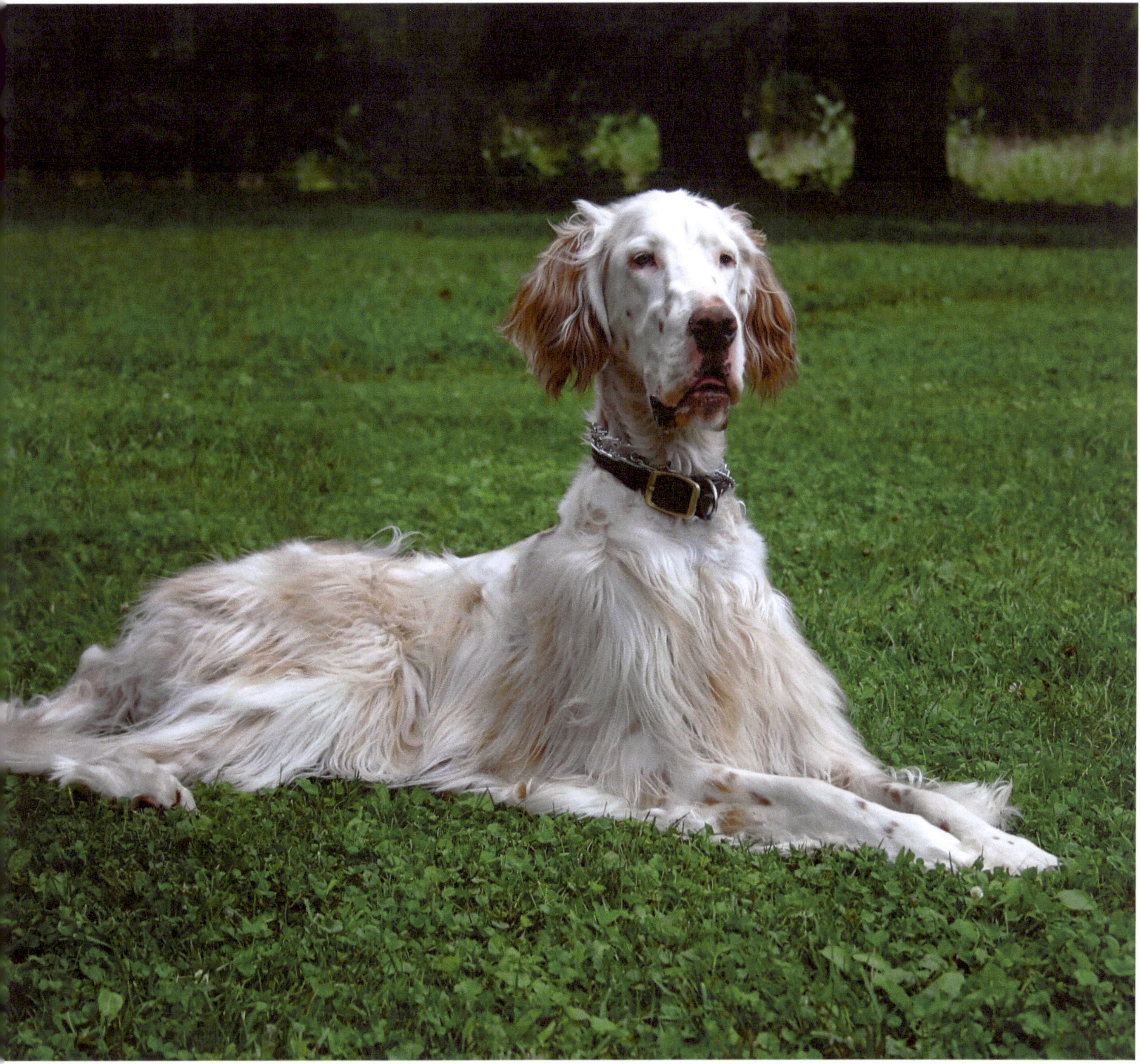

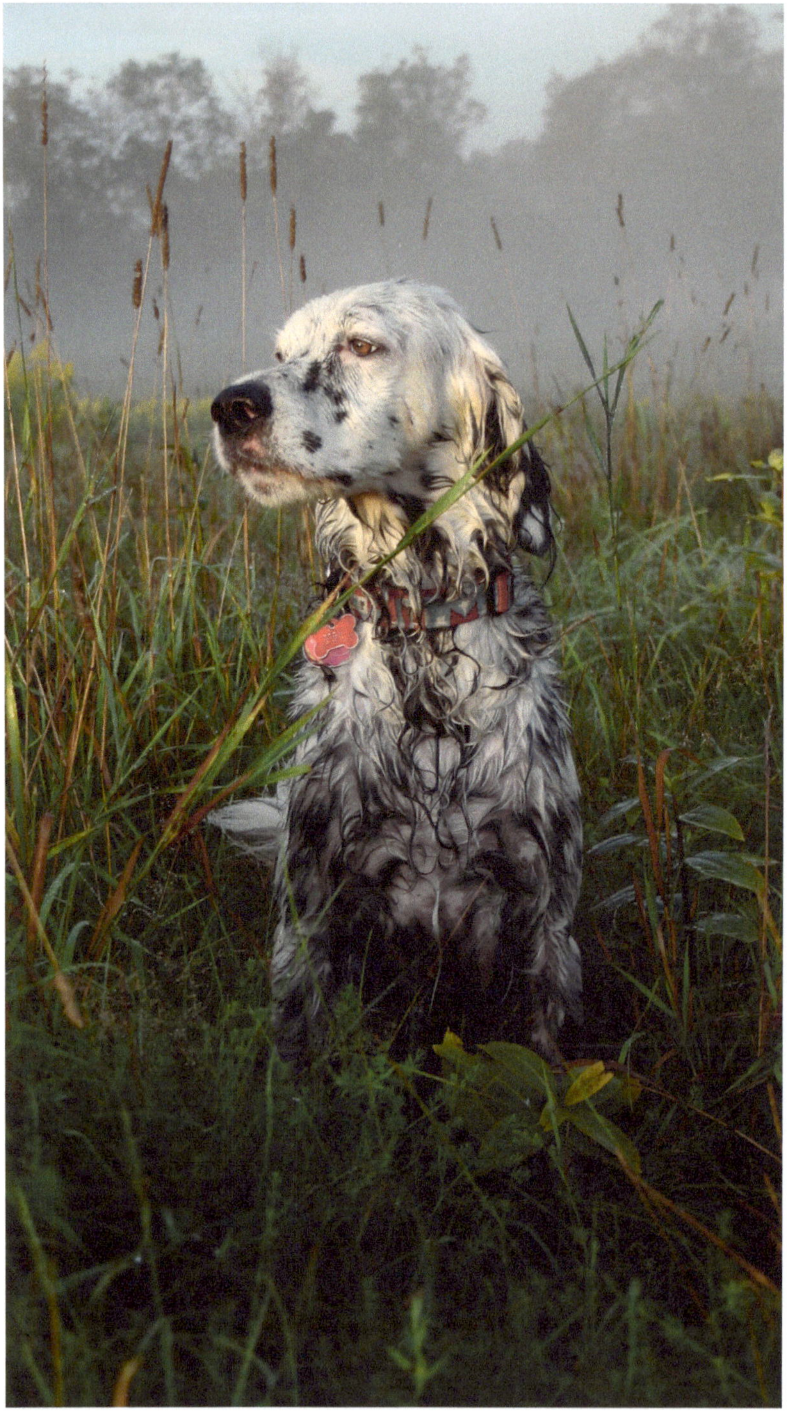

Llewellin Setters are English Setters from breeding lines developed by Richard L. Purcell Llewellin, Esq. (1840-1925). Llewellins are registered in the Field Dog Stud Book (FDSB) instead of by the AKC, and must be descended from Llewellin's original stock. There have been several unsuccessful attempts by the Llewellin breeding community to get the Llewellin Setter recognized as a separate breed from the English Setter since the AKC registered version bears little resemblance to the Llewellin Setter. Llewellins have shorter coats than the bench dogs and smaller flews; their energy levels are much higher since they are used actively as working gun dogs across the US.

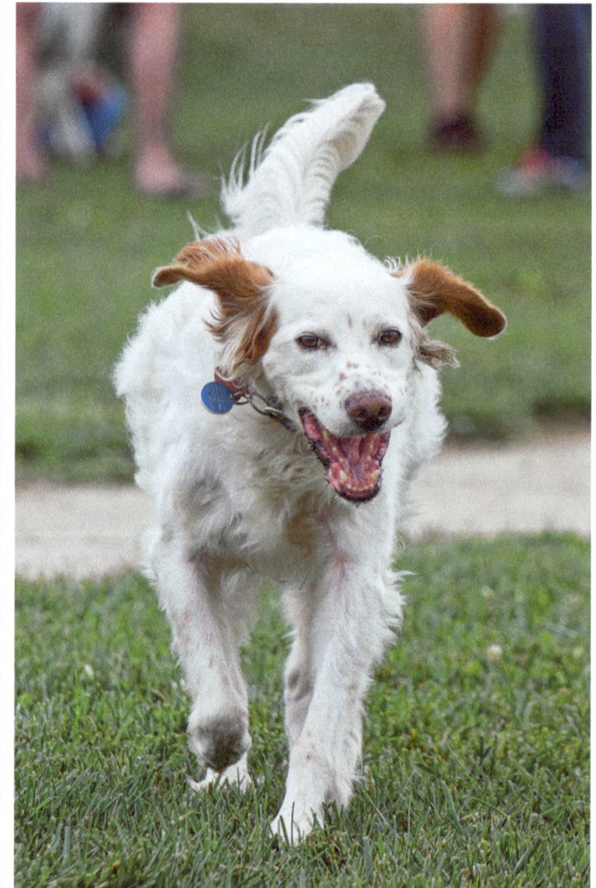

The "field type" English Setter is descended mostly from Llewellin's breeding lines in the United States. There is more variety in terms of size, shape, and color in the field type English Setter because hunting ability trumps most physical characteristics. These dogs are also registered in the FDSB but no specific breeding lines are required. Field dogs are usually smaller than bench and Llwellins and can run anywhere from 25lb "pocket" Setters to larger 50lb dogs. These are active, high-energy dogs, who can keep up with hunters, both on foot and on horseback, and range far for hours on end.

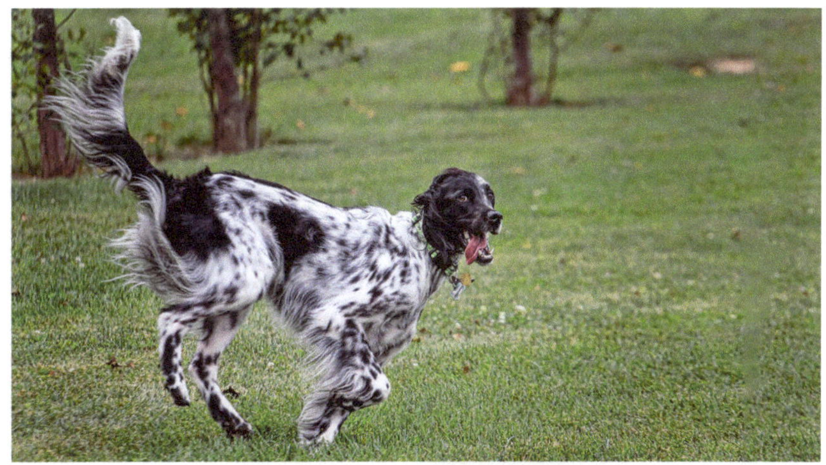

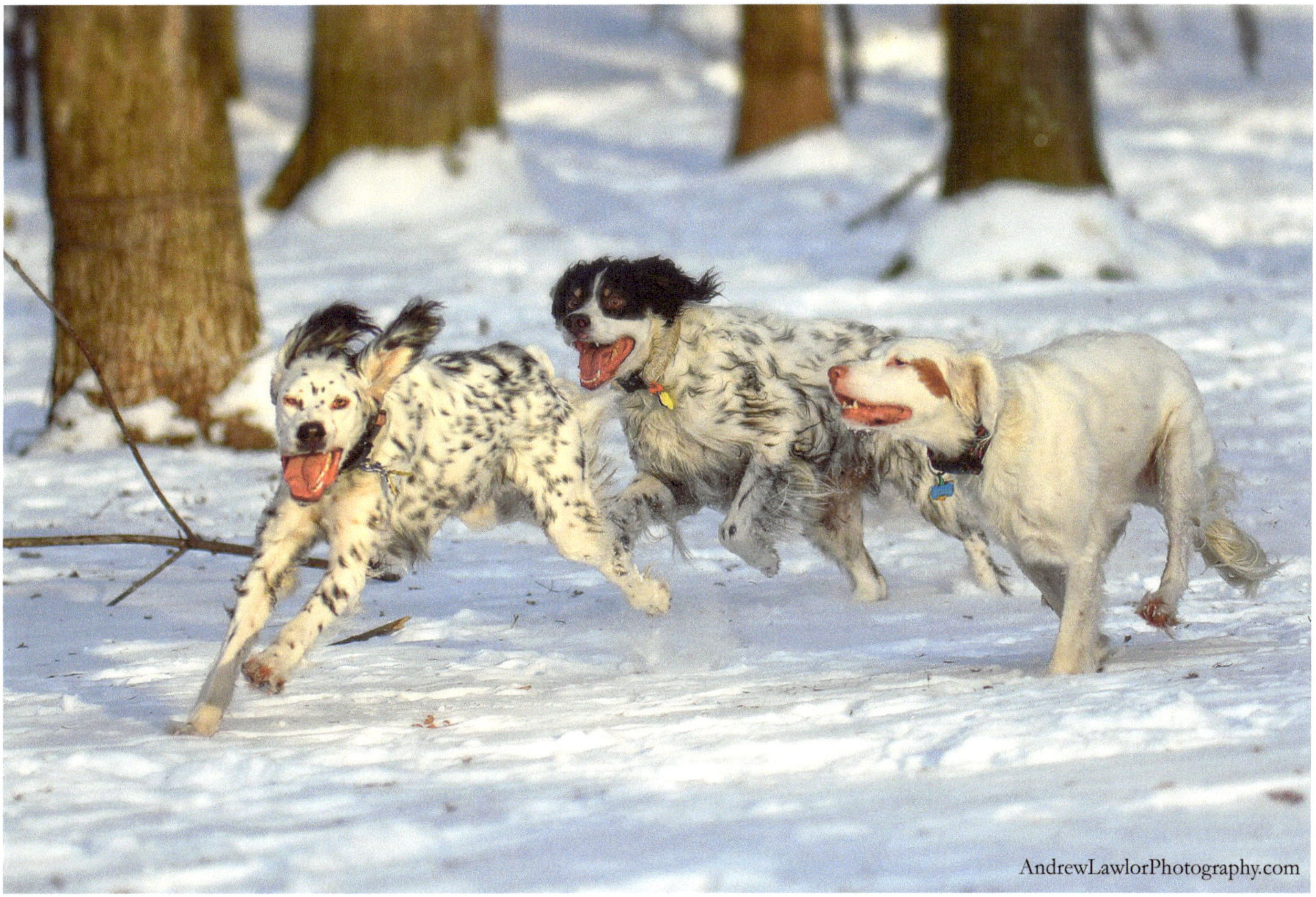

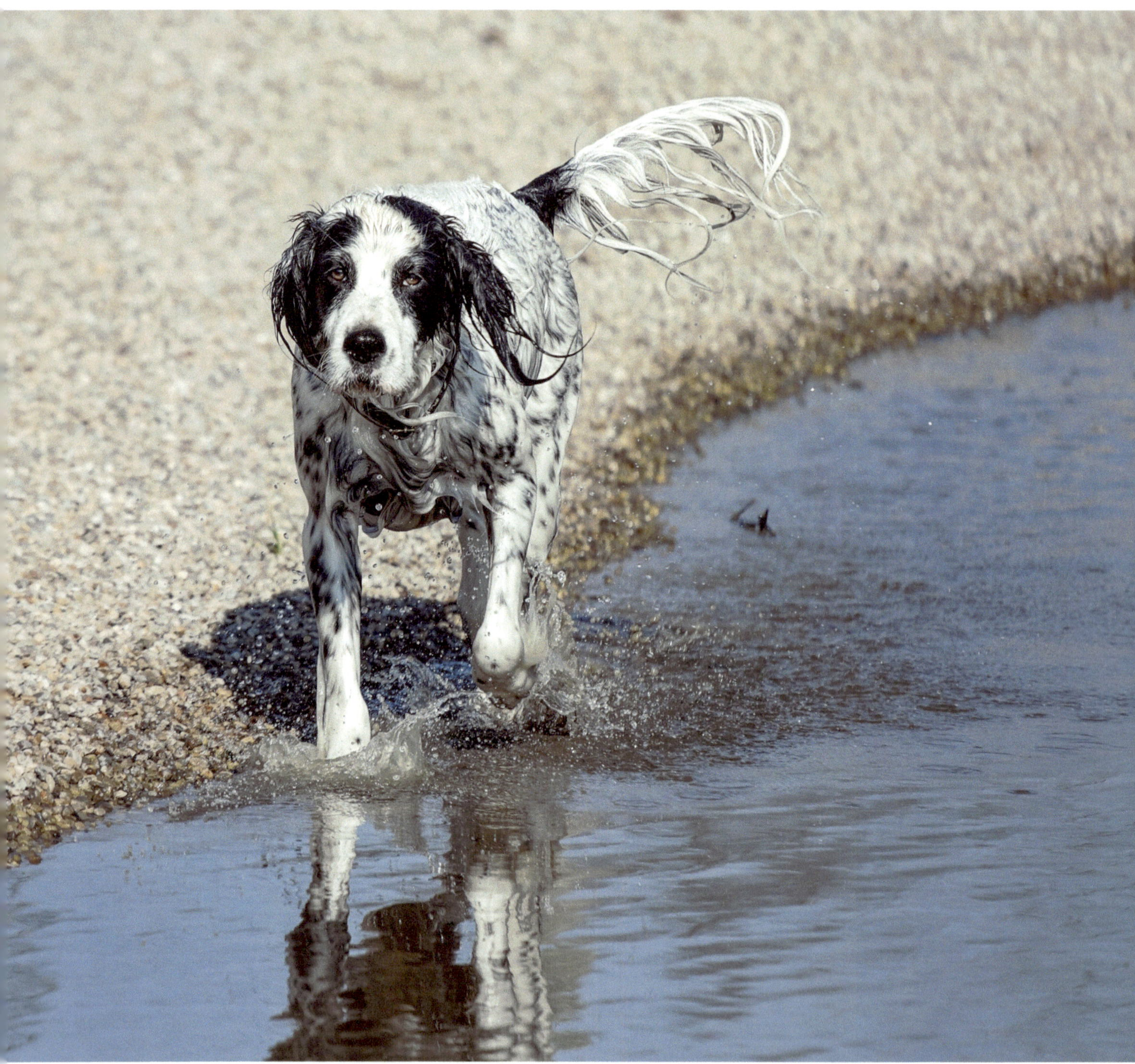

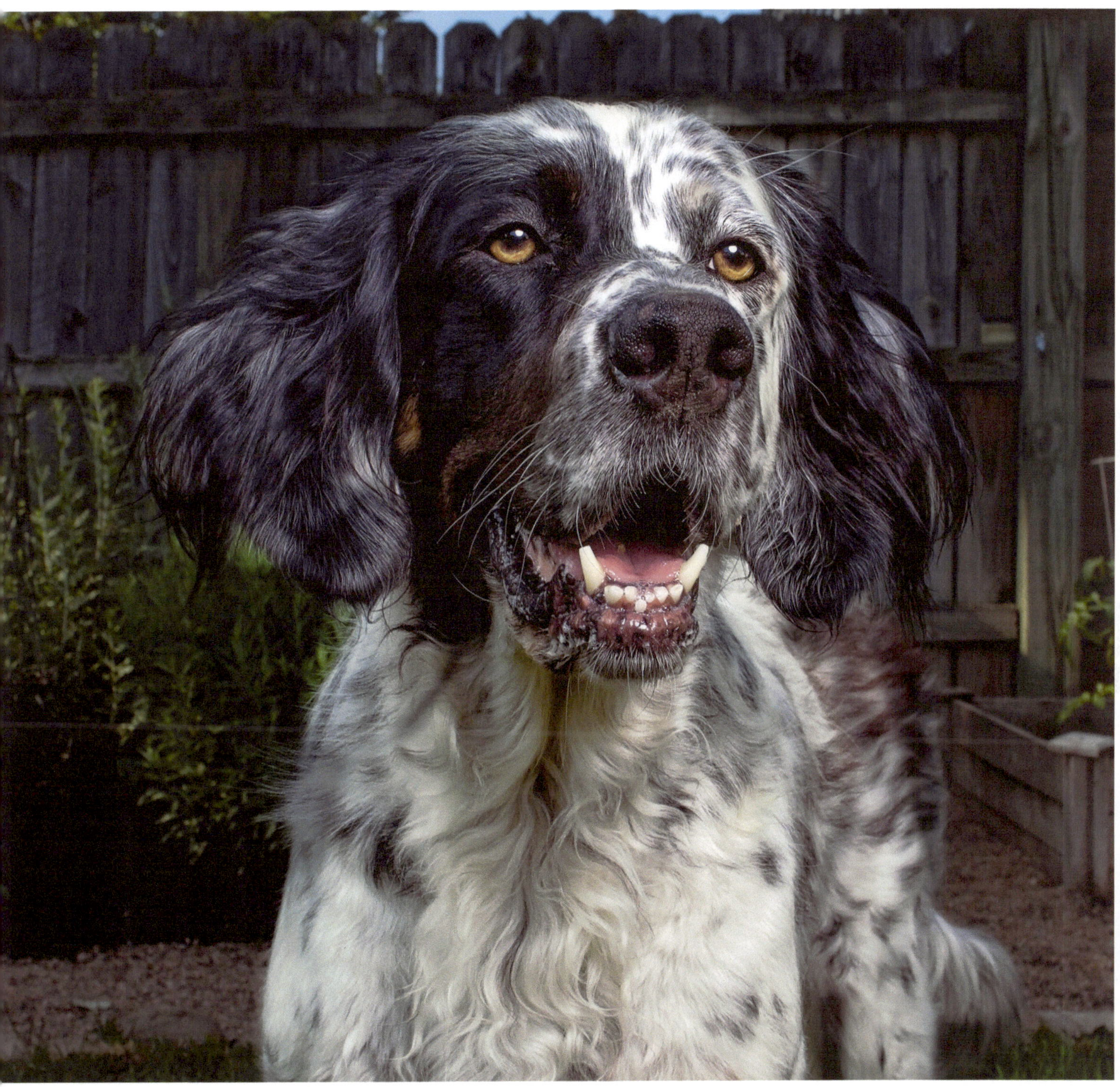

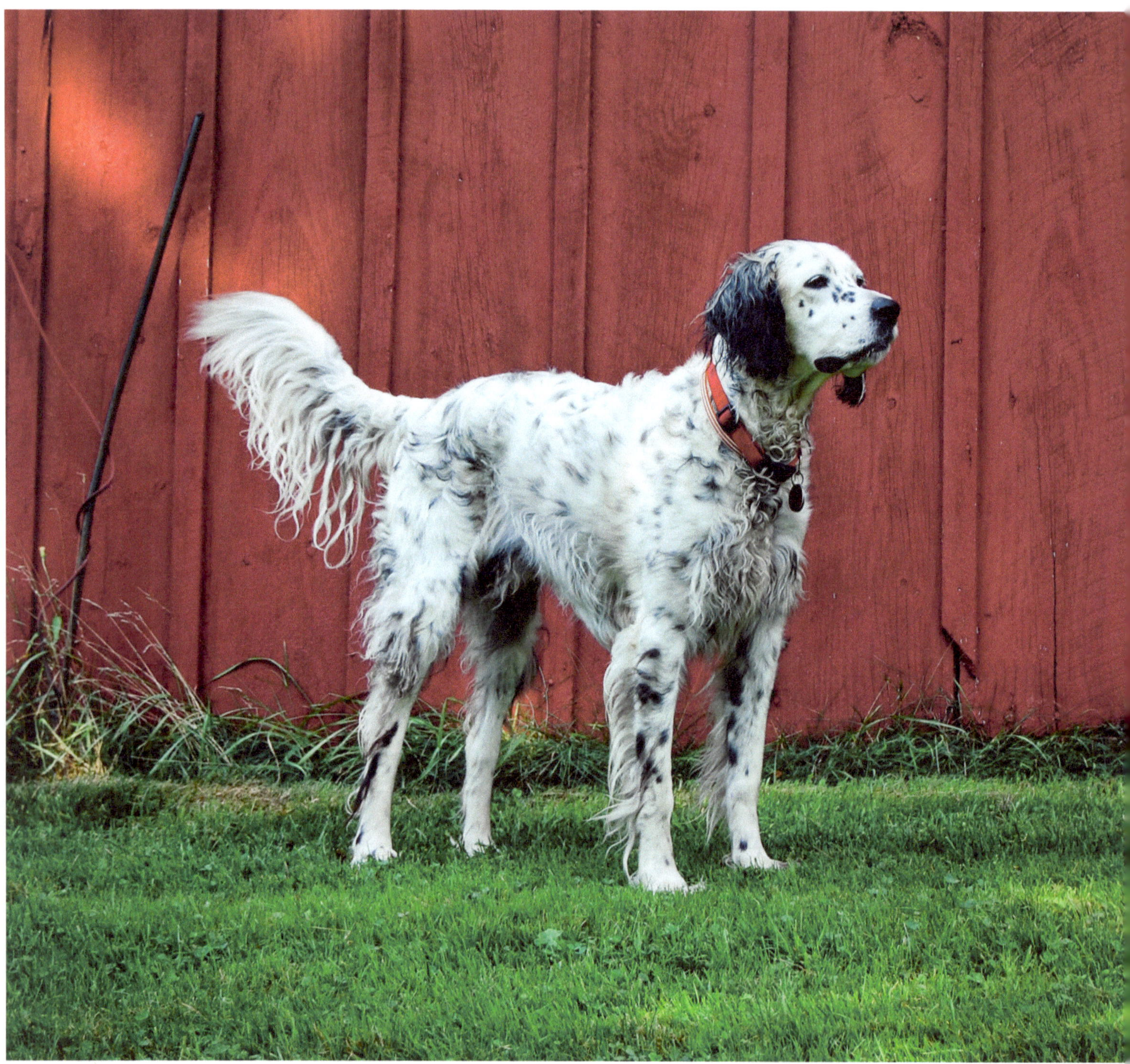

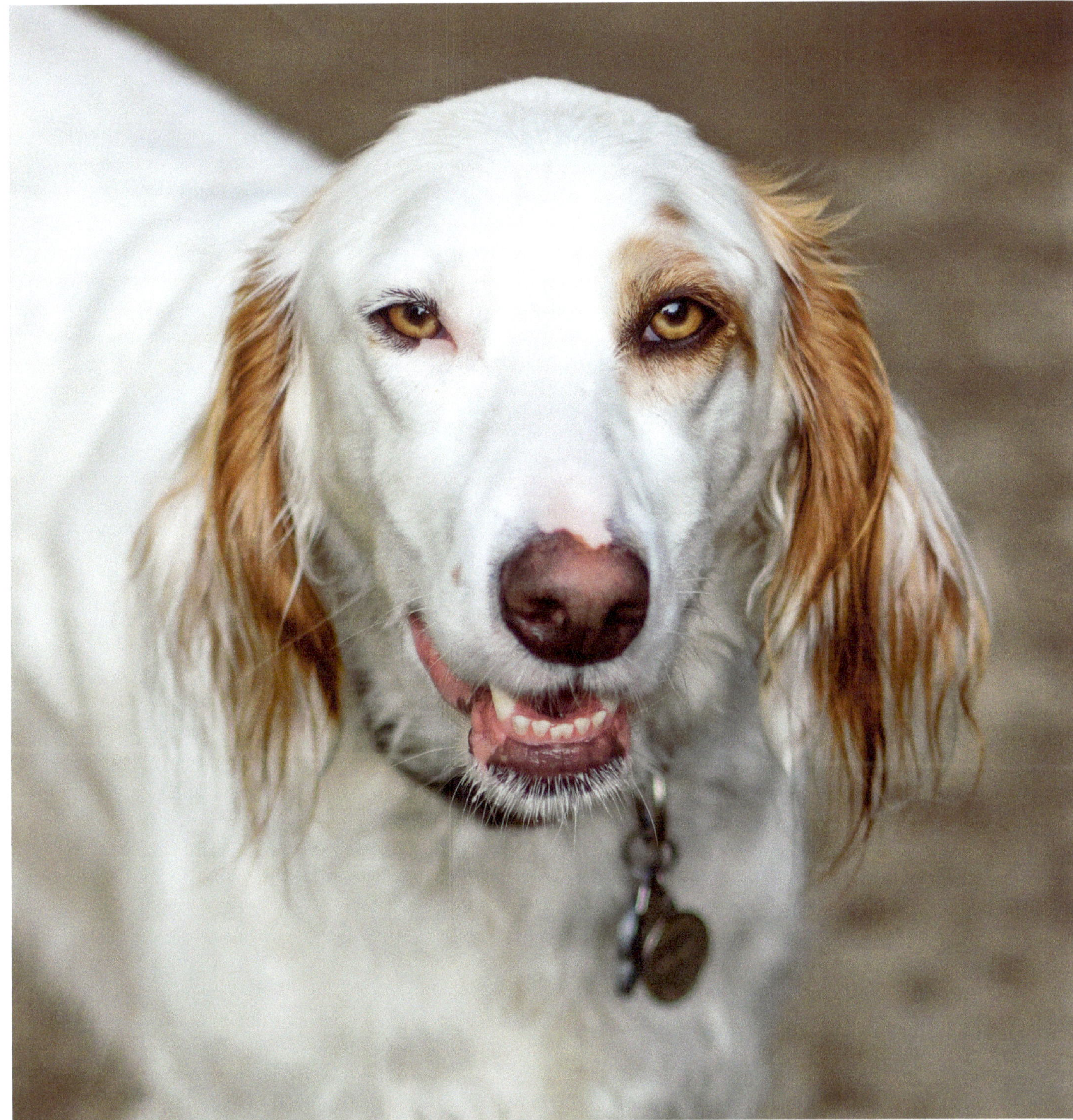

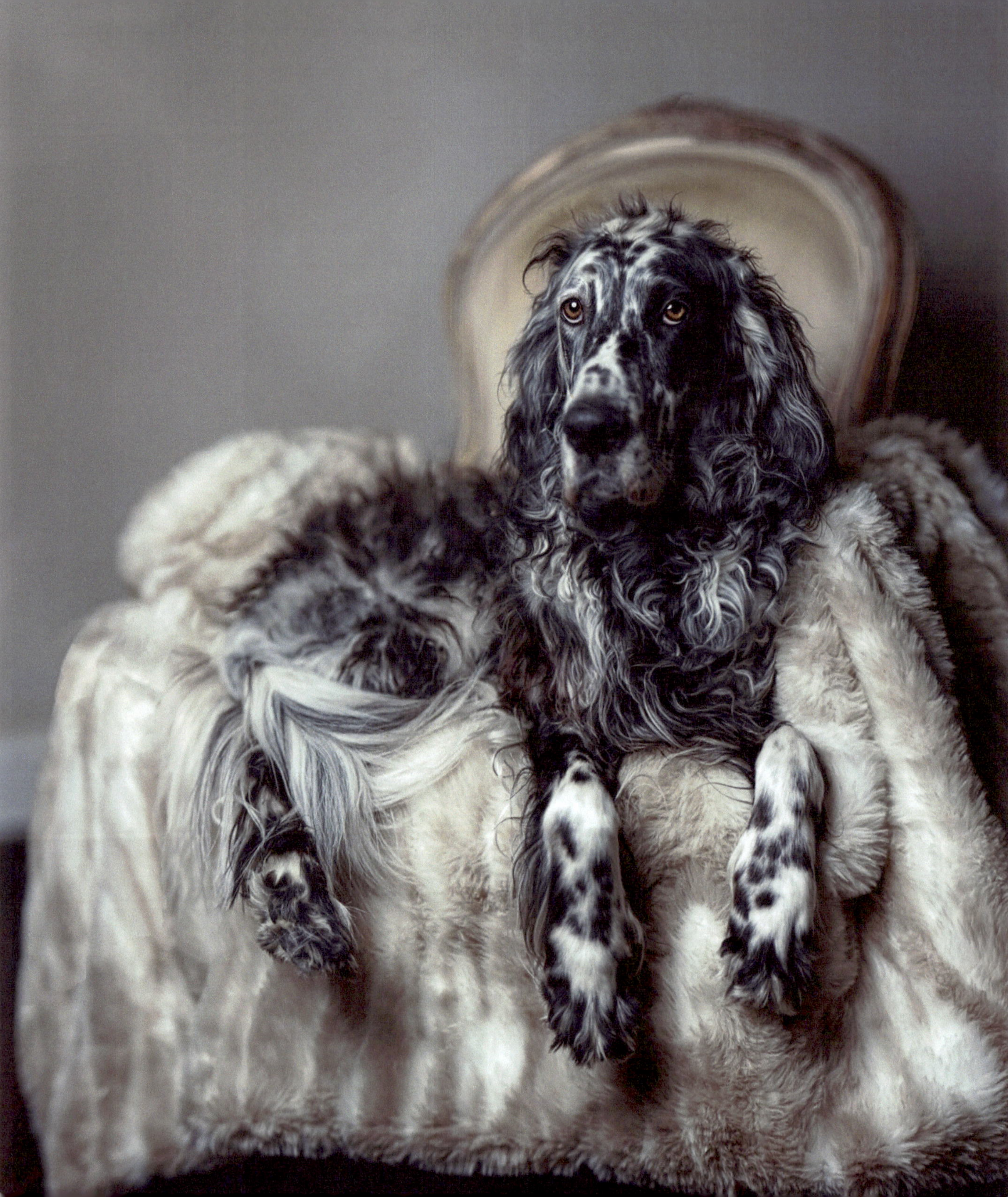

In the United States, a fourth type developed by George Ryman bridged the widening gap between the bench dogs and the field dogs, by breeding them both together to get a good-looking dog that can also work well in the field. These dogs are called "Ryman English Setters" or "Rymans" and can be both AKC and FDSB registered. Rymans are larger dogs, males sometimes reaching 75lbs. They are prized for their closer foot hunting and balanced energy levels.

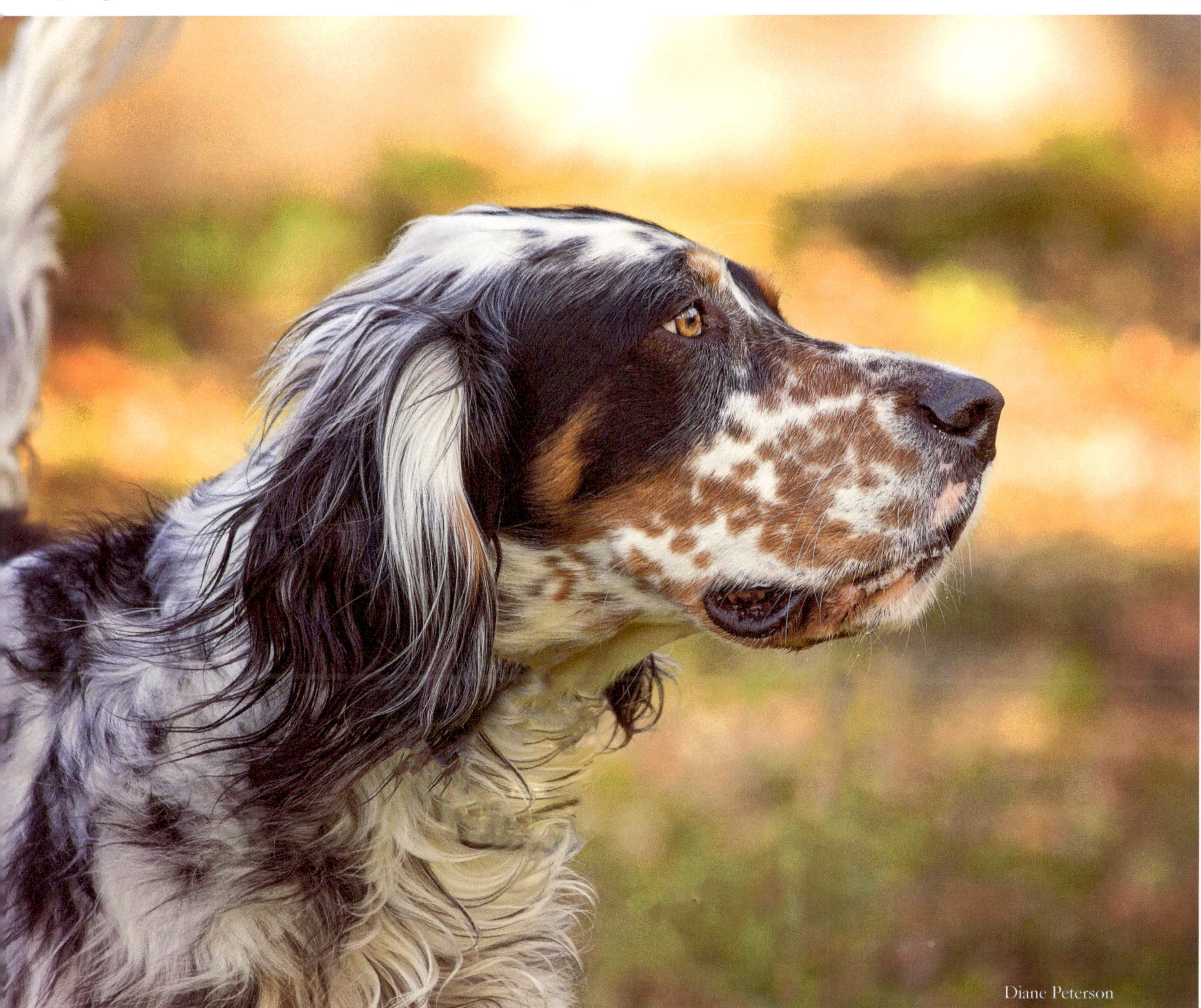

English Setters have spots that come in several different colors - black, orange, lemon, brown, and tri-colored (two different colors on a white coat). Some English Setters have a lot of little spots and some just have a few big ones. Some barely have any spots at all and some have so many they're almost solid! The spot pattern is called "belton" and you'll hear Setters described as "Blue Belton" (black and white) or "Orange Belton" (orange and white) and so on. English Setter puppies are born mostly white and it's difficult to tell how many spots they'll have or what color they are. However many spots they have or what color, they are all English Setters.

These beautiful dogs are not very common in parts of the United States and some people think they are Dalmatians or Dalmatian mixes but the two breeds are not related. The only thing they have in common is their pretty spots.

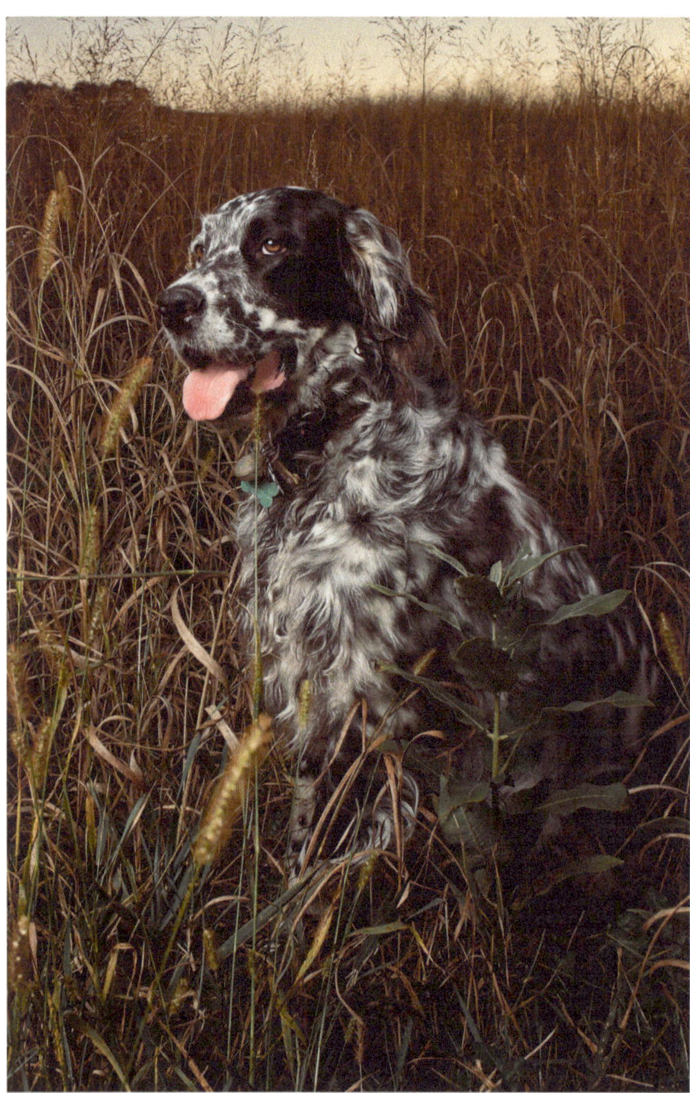

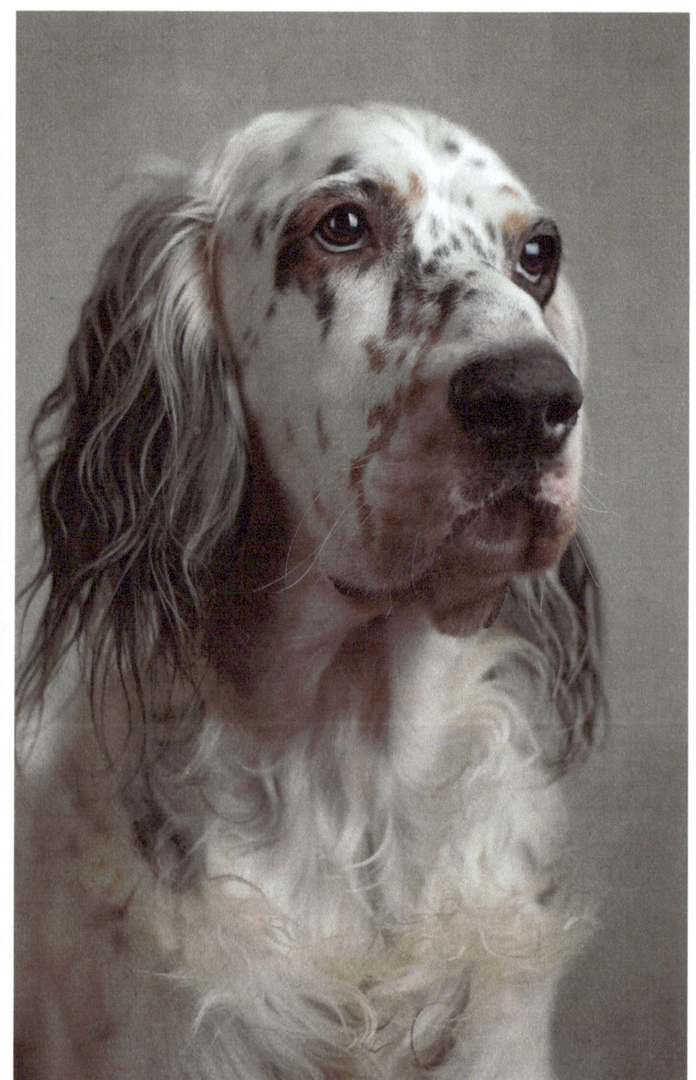

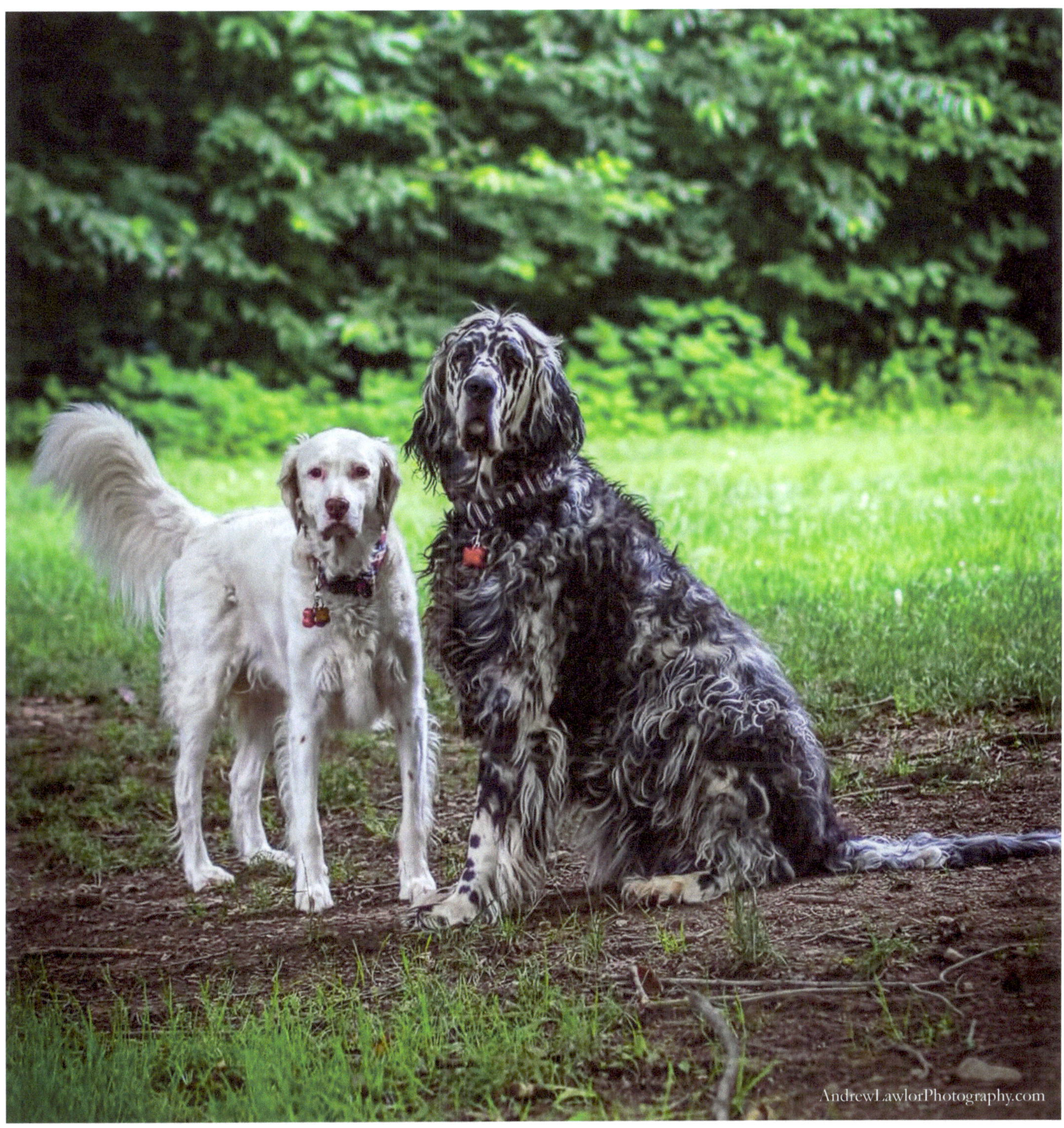
AndrewLawlorPhotography.com

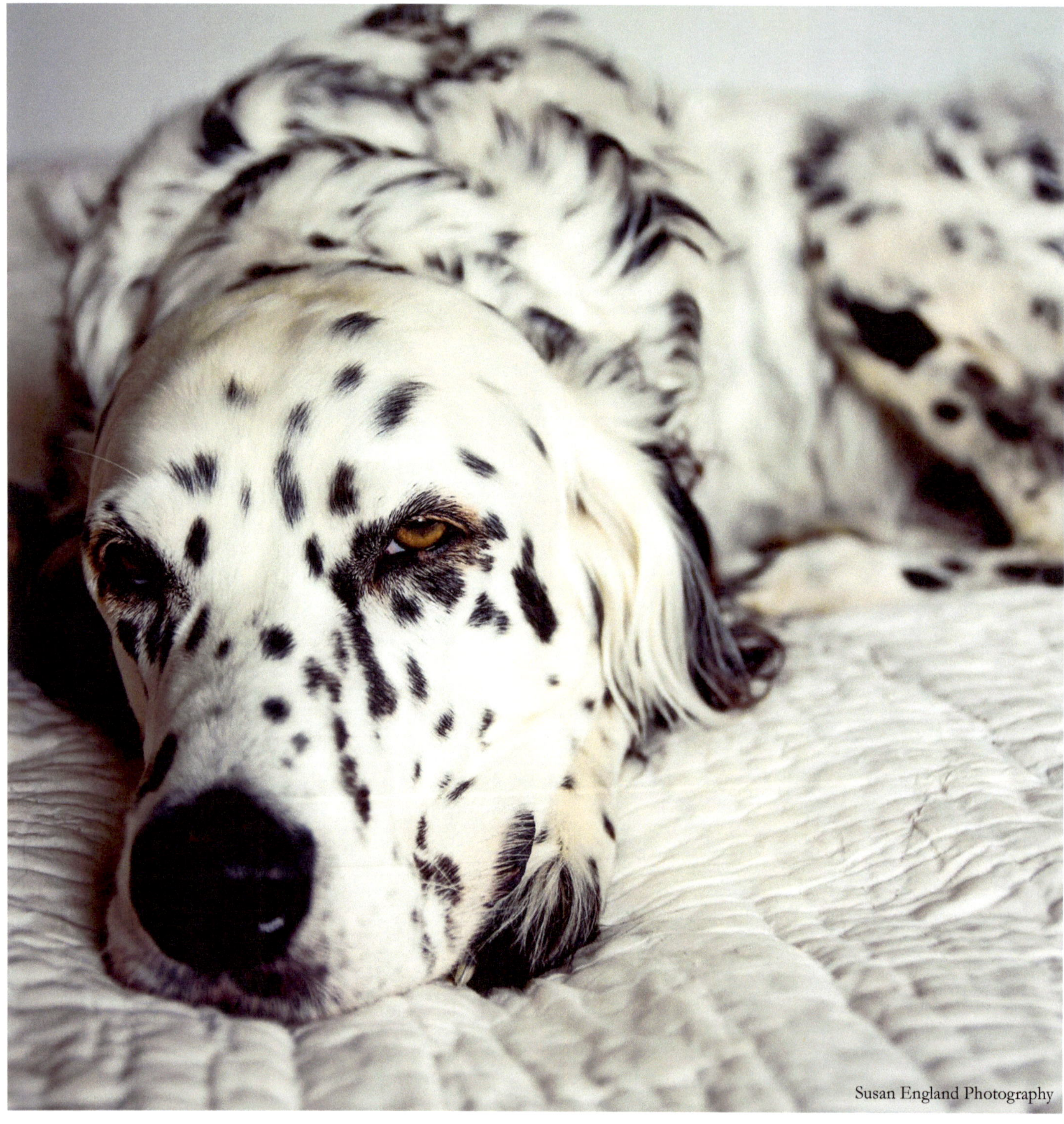

Susan England Photography

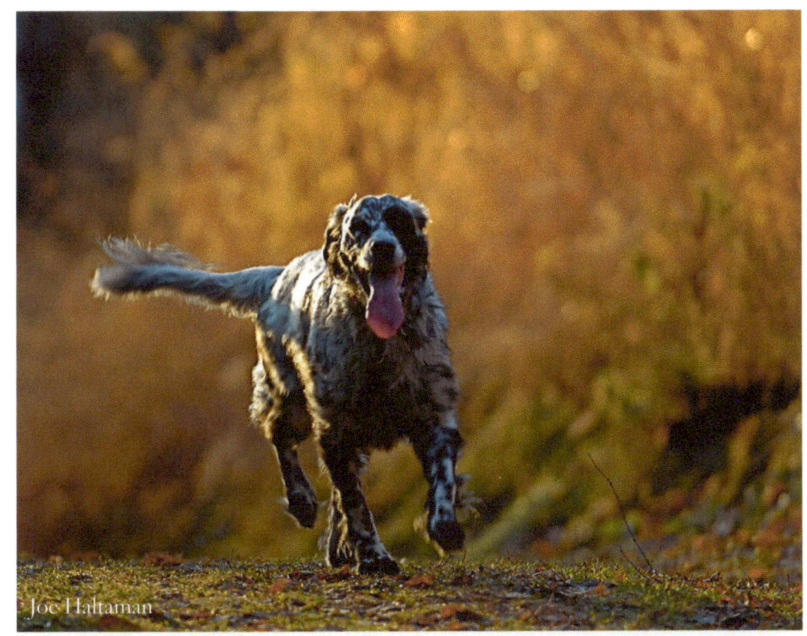
Joe Haltaman

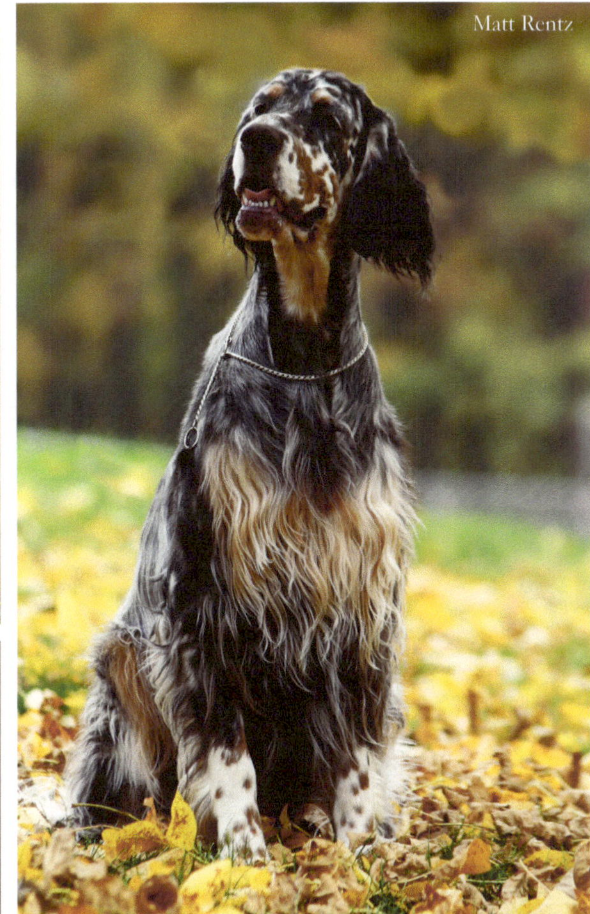
Matt Rentz

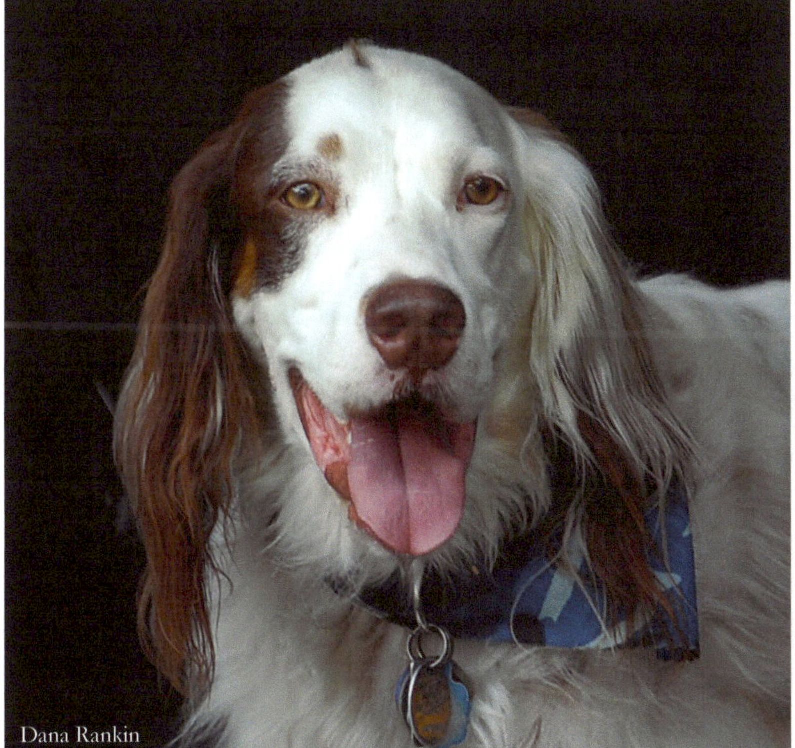
Dana Rankin

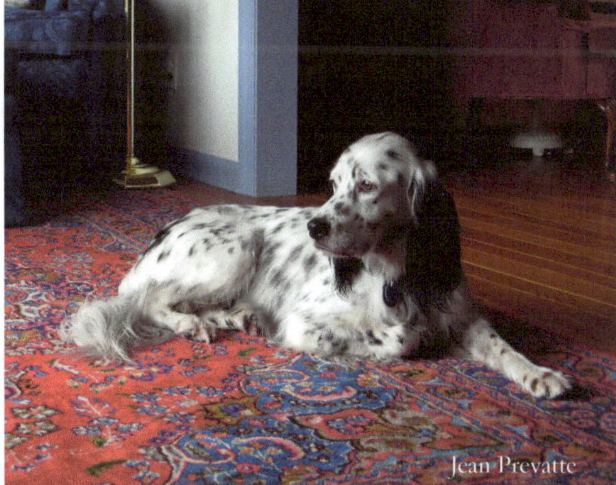
Jean Prevatte

What are they Like?

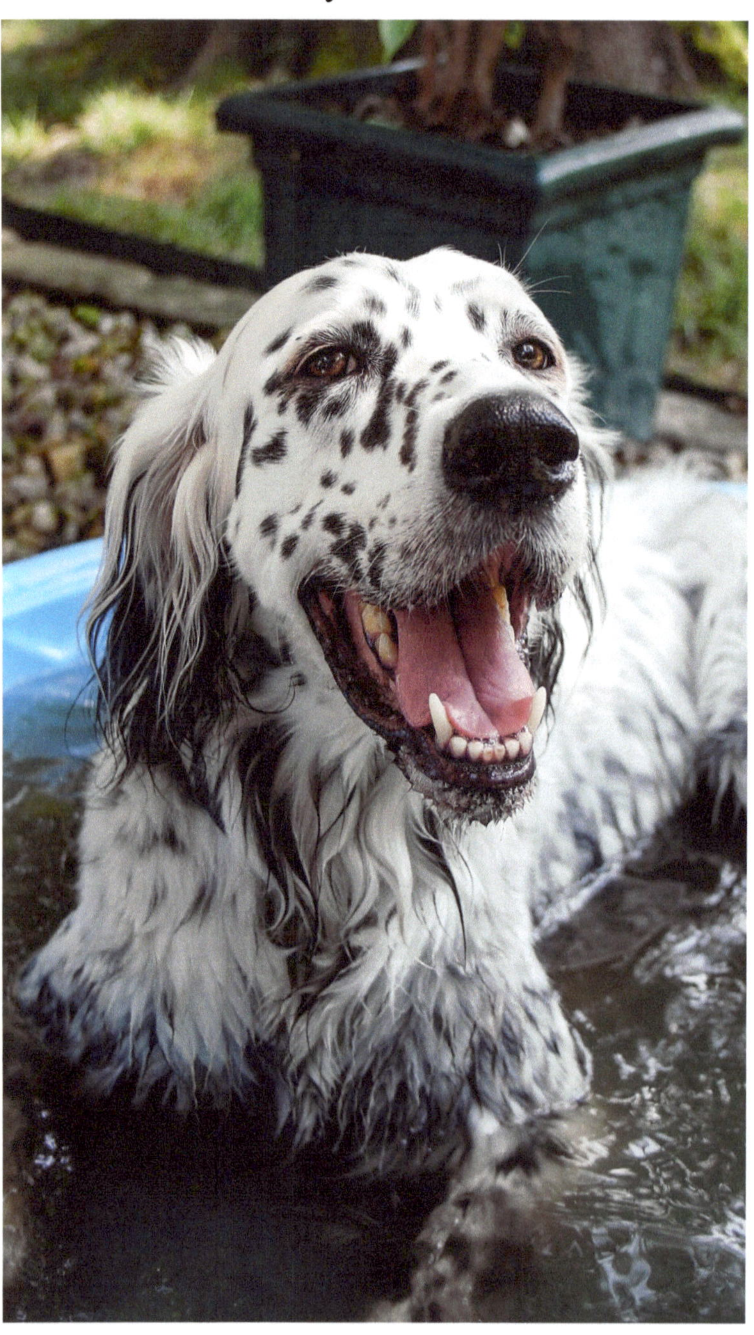

Just like people, every dog has a different personality that's influenced by their genetics and their environment. People have been breeding Setters for over 600 hundred years to behave in a certain way so we can make some generalizations about them even though each dog is an individual.

English Setters are very affectionate and bond strongly with their family members. That loyalty helps to make certain that they don't run off when they're out hunting. They also need to be able to work independently from the hunters, ranging as far as a mile away looking for hidden birds, so they've got minds of their own. This can make for some very interesting situations which can either leave you with really high blood pressure or laughing hysterically! Their goofy antics will definitely keep you entertained. They're pretty good at manipulating people, too; those big soulful eyes are great for begging.

Setters are supposed to be able to work all day in the fields running around and looking for birds. This can translate into a dog that needs a lot of exercise and stares all day at your neighbor's bird bath. Setters get bored and a change of scenery is a great way to distract them. Even a quick walk around the block can help bleed off some nervous energy. You don't need three acres and game birds in your yard to keep a Setter happy. A reasonable amount of daily exercise and an occasional run at the dog park will keep most setters settled down in the house and happy to be your personal lap warmers. A fenced backyard is a must. English Setters can travel a long way in very little time and if they're focused on some small prey, staying close to home may not be their highest priority. They may listen great 95% of the time but it's that other 5% that lands a large number of English Setters in animal shelters.

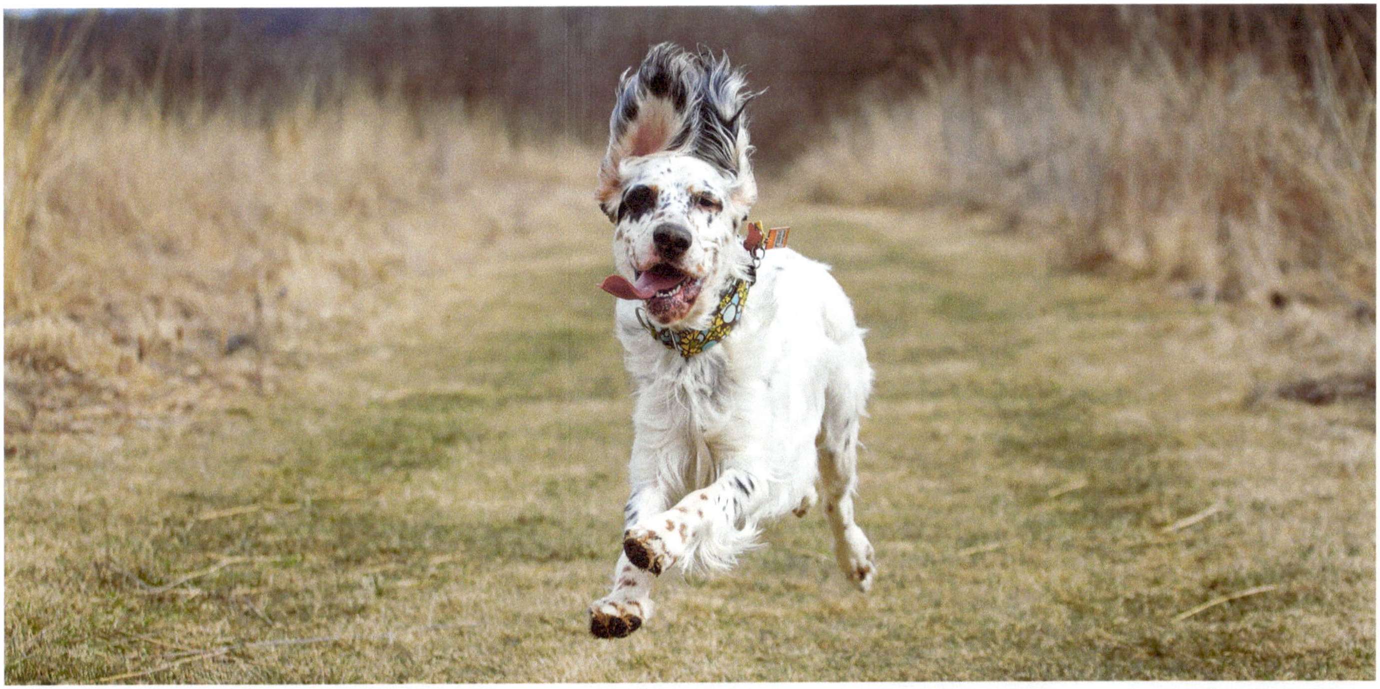

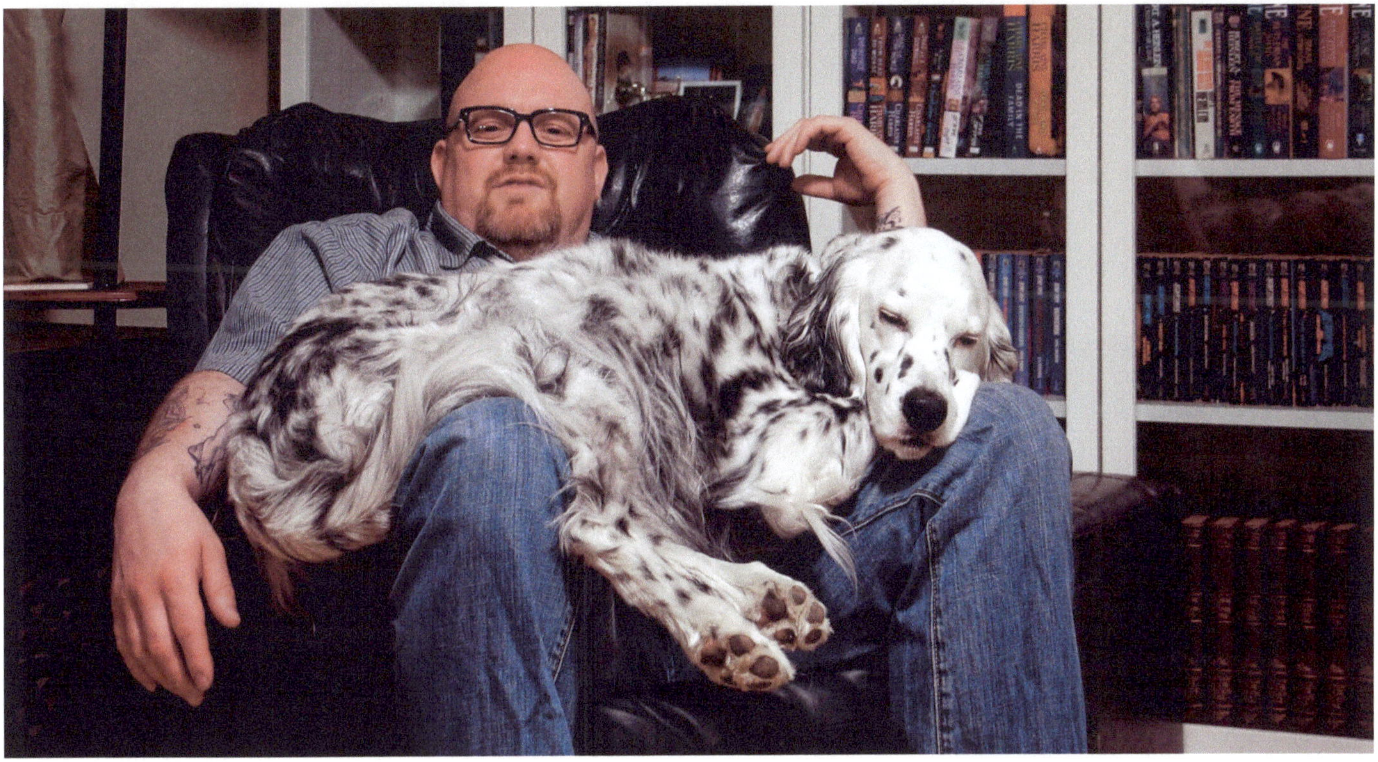

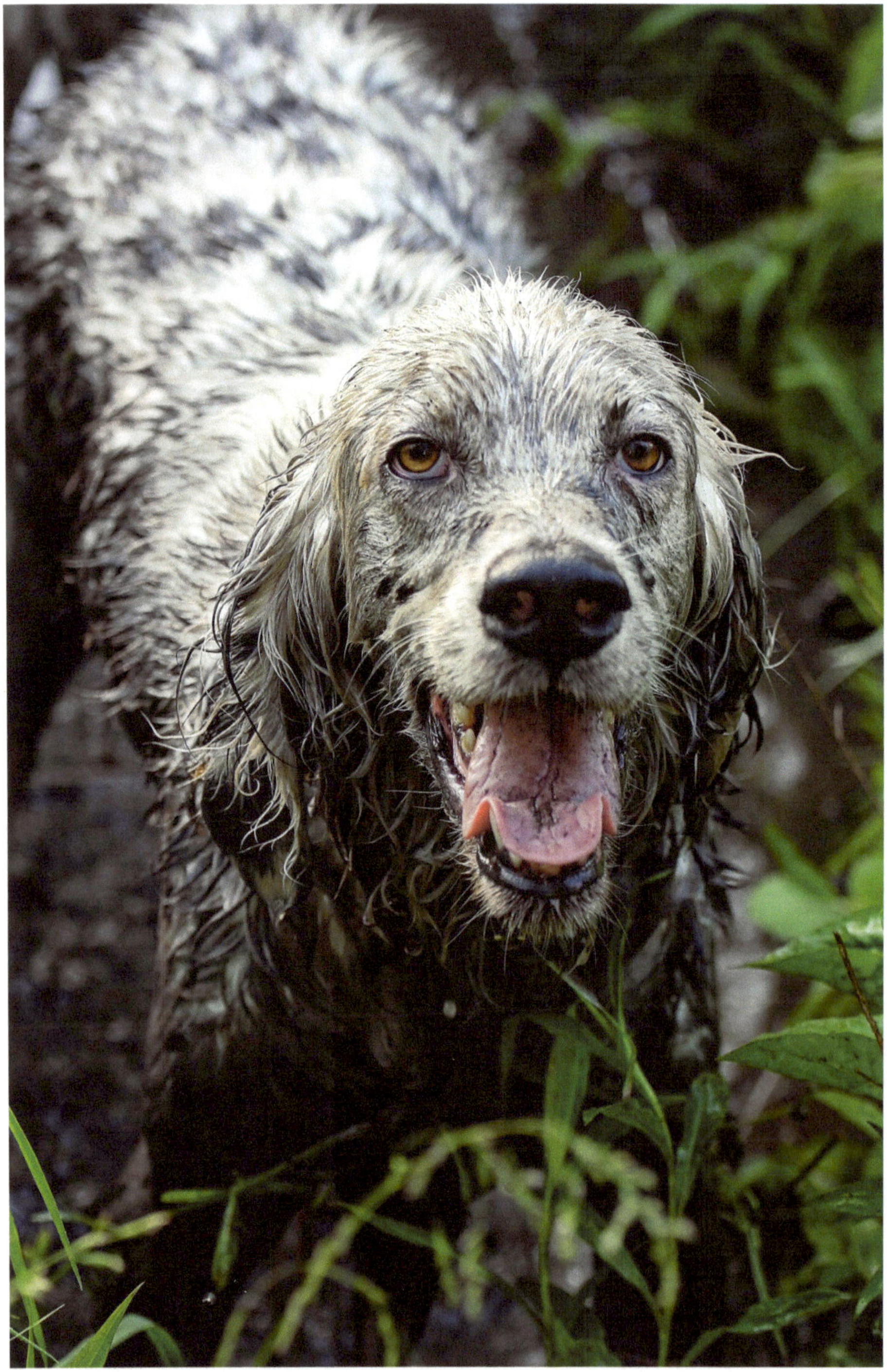

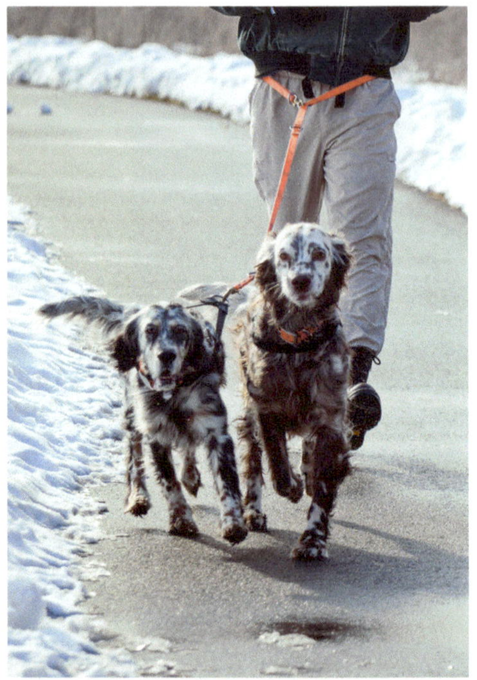

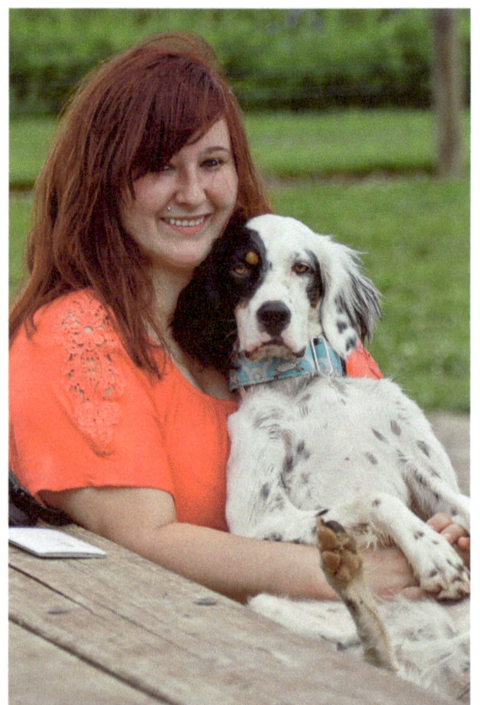

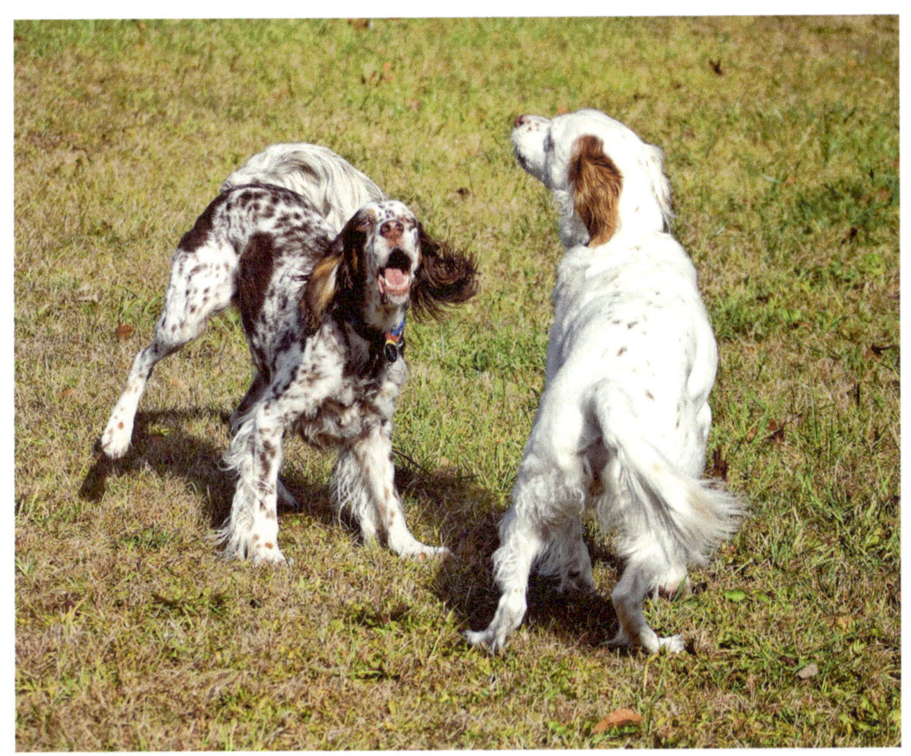

English Setters are gentle, sweet, sensitive, and thrive on love and companionship. They are generally friendly and fit in very well as family dogs. Although their energy levels may be a bit too much for very young children, there are plenty of families who find that they fit in perfectly.

English Setters are considered "soft dogs" by trainers. That means that they do not take well to harsh corrections. You will get better consistent results by using patience and positive training methods. If you're not hunting your Setter, consider some fun agility, rally, or obedience classes. They learn fast, are eager to please, and giving their brains a work-out is just as important as physical activity. A bored Setter will find something with which to entertain themselves and it's usually not something you're going to like!

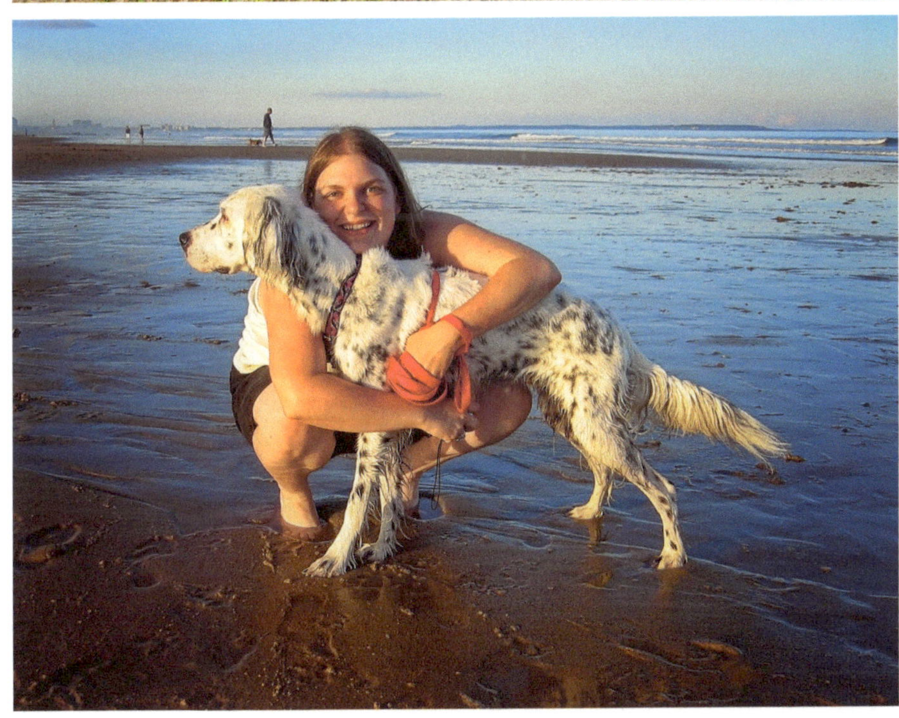

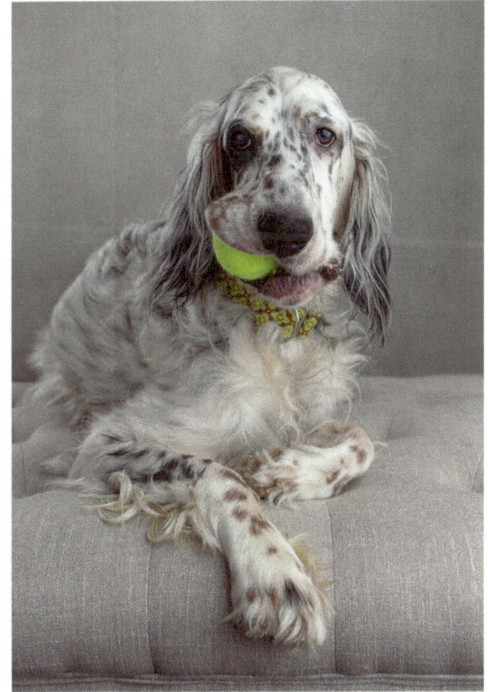

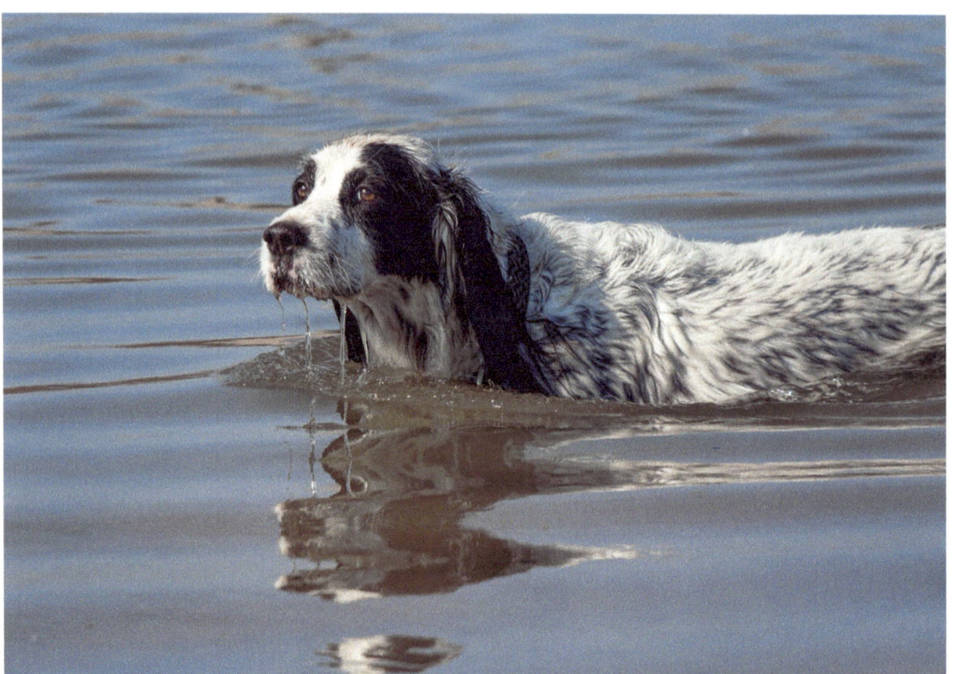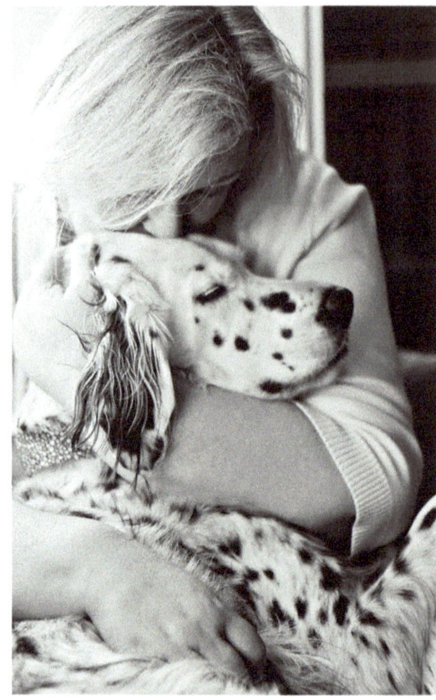

Their beautiful coats are very soft and are a joy to pet and pretty easy to maintain. Mud dries and falls off and, since these are not water dogs, they don't get a "doggy smell" when they get wet. That was a nice surprise for me after having owned retrievers for many years! As they get older, their coats often start to get curly, especially on the longer coated dogs.

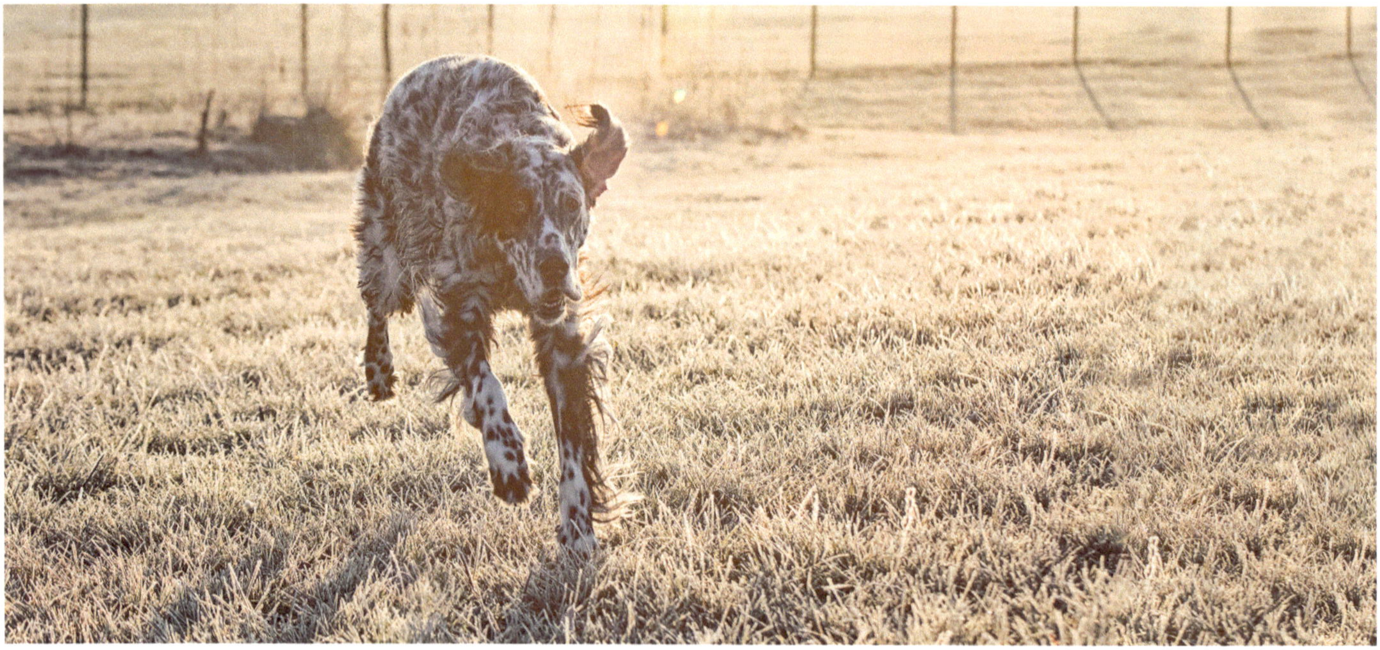

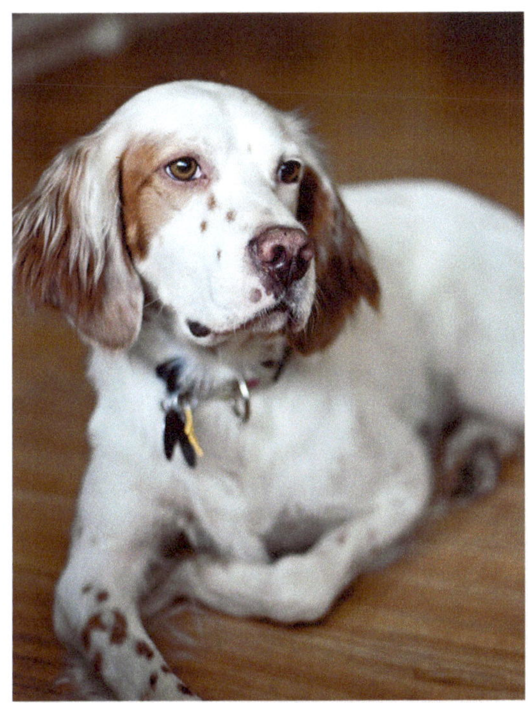

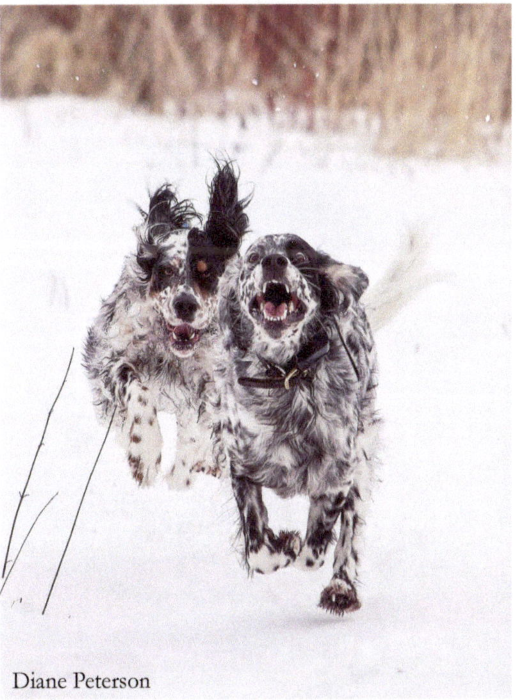

Diane Peterson

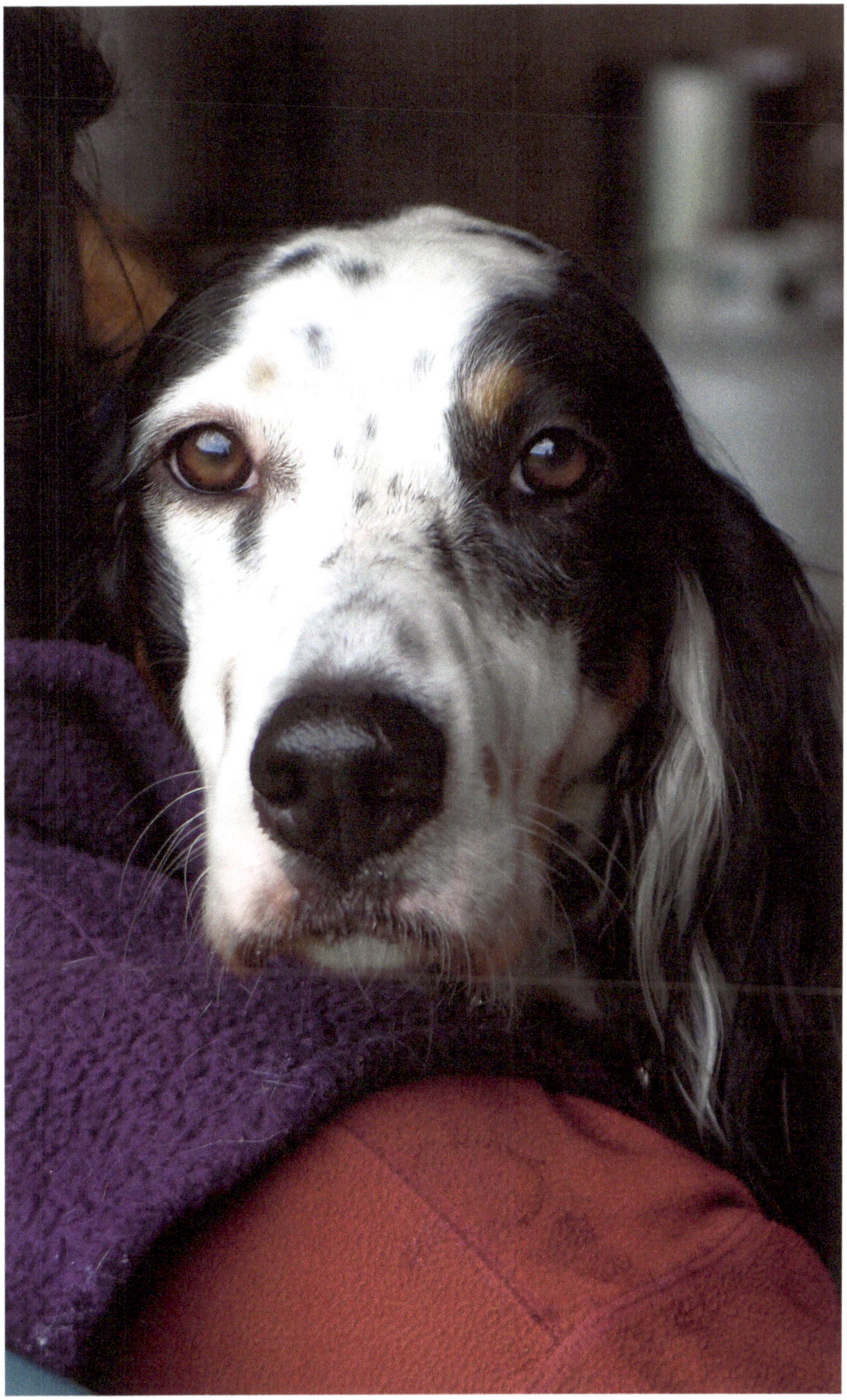

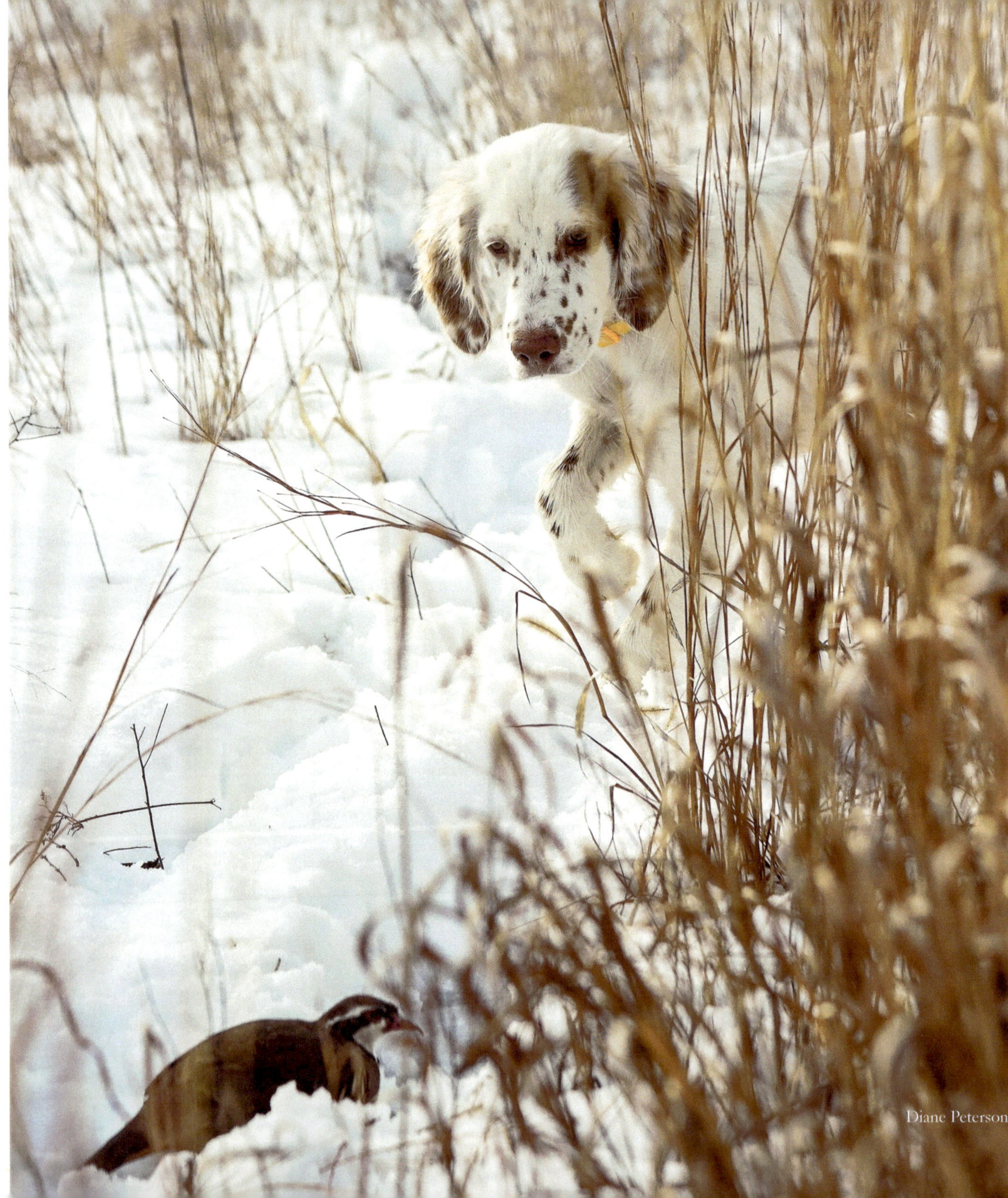
Diane Peterson

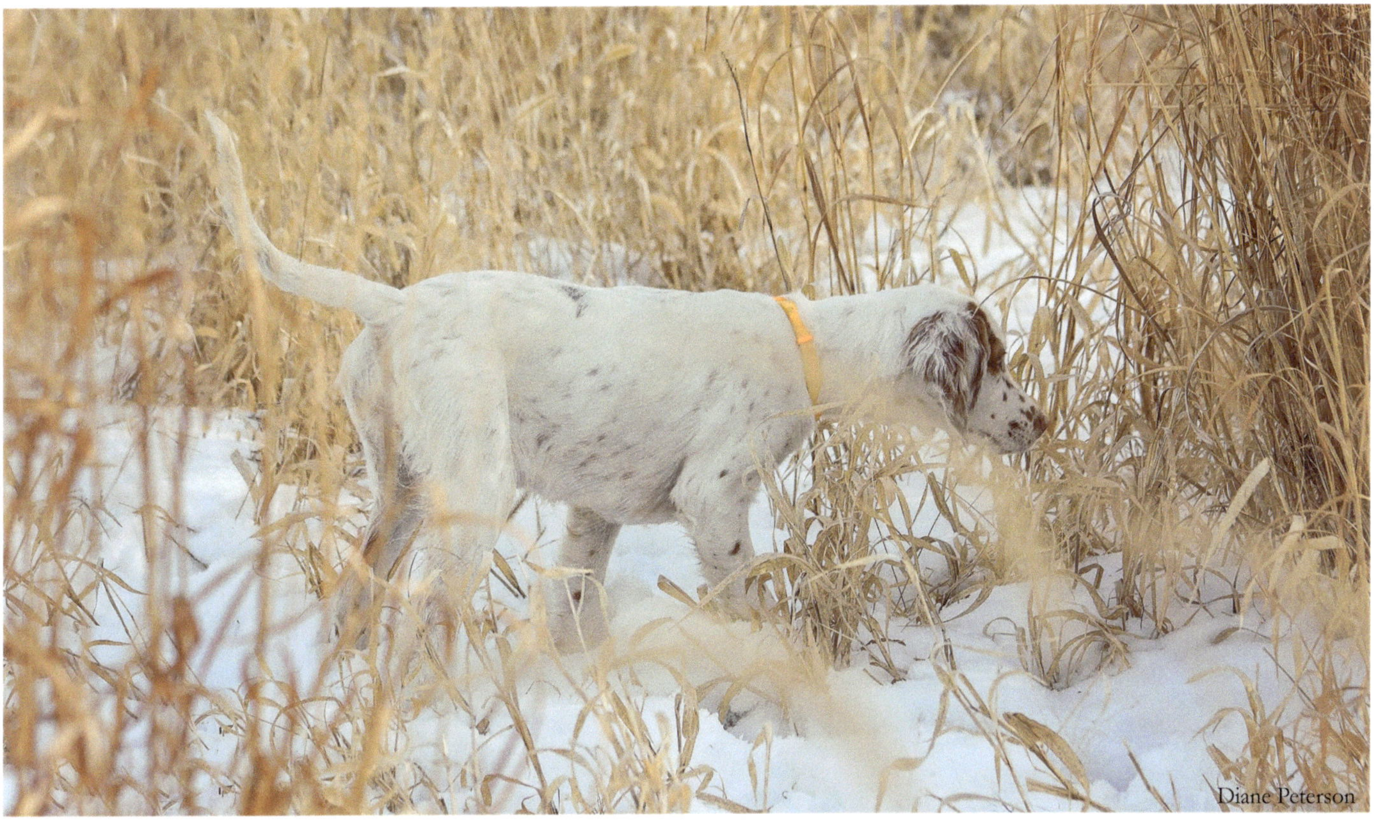

The "bird dog instinct" is strong in English Setters. Even young puppies will show off their hunting abilities when presented with the right stimuli. The puppies in these photographs are only twelve weeks old and are already displaying the skills for which they've been bred for over 600 years.

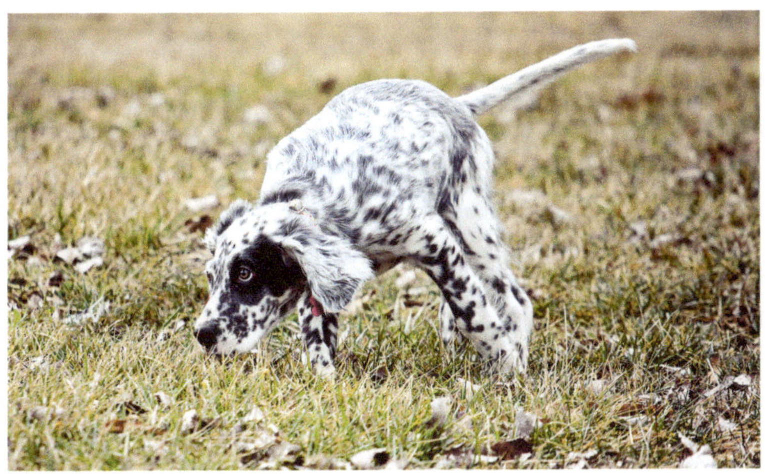

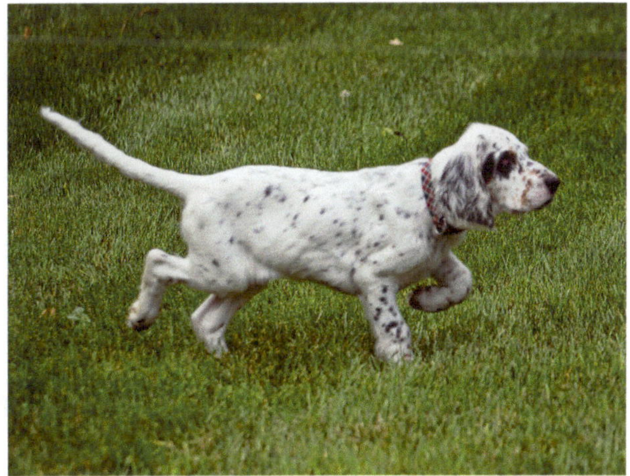

The Versatile Setter

English Setters are a very adaptable breed. Although they are bred to be upland hunting dogs, their close proximity to their handlers means that they are eager to please and are pleasant companion dogs. English Setters can do more than just hunt. They can do agility, obedience, tracking, be therapy dogs, search and rescue… the list is endless. Here are a few examples:

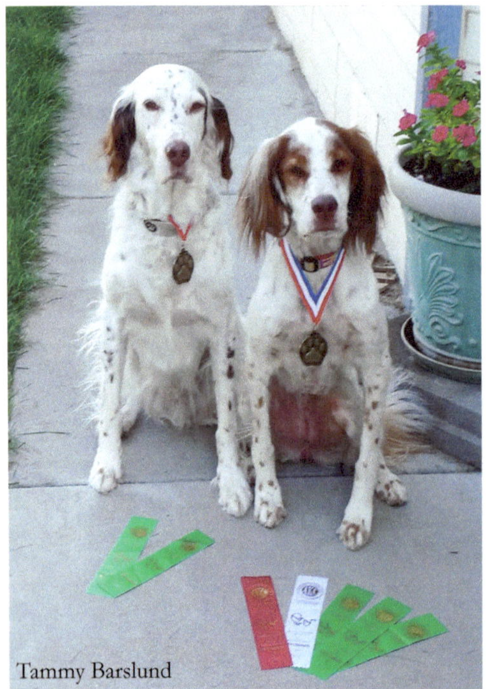

Tammy Barslund

Titus and Tessa are good at Obedience

Kathy Goodwin

Gromit works as a therapy dog at the Los Angeles airport

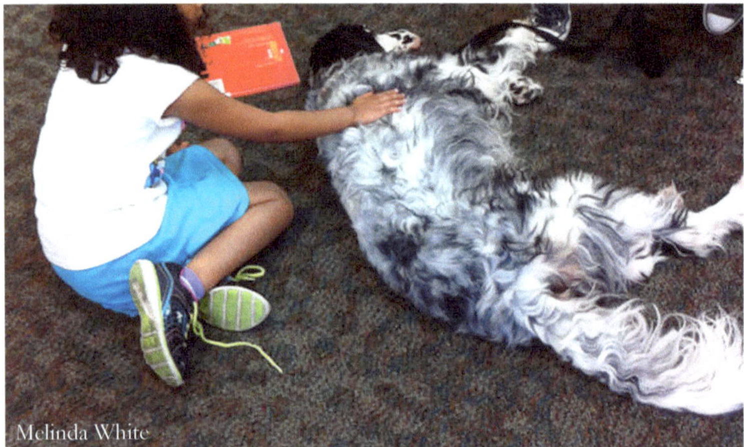

Melinda White

Will is really relaxed during a reading therapy session

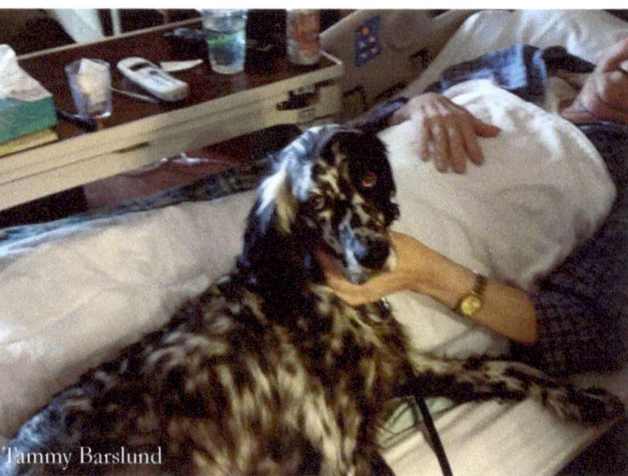

Tammy Barslund

Levi brings a smile during a therapy session

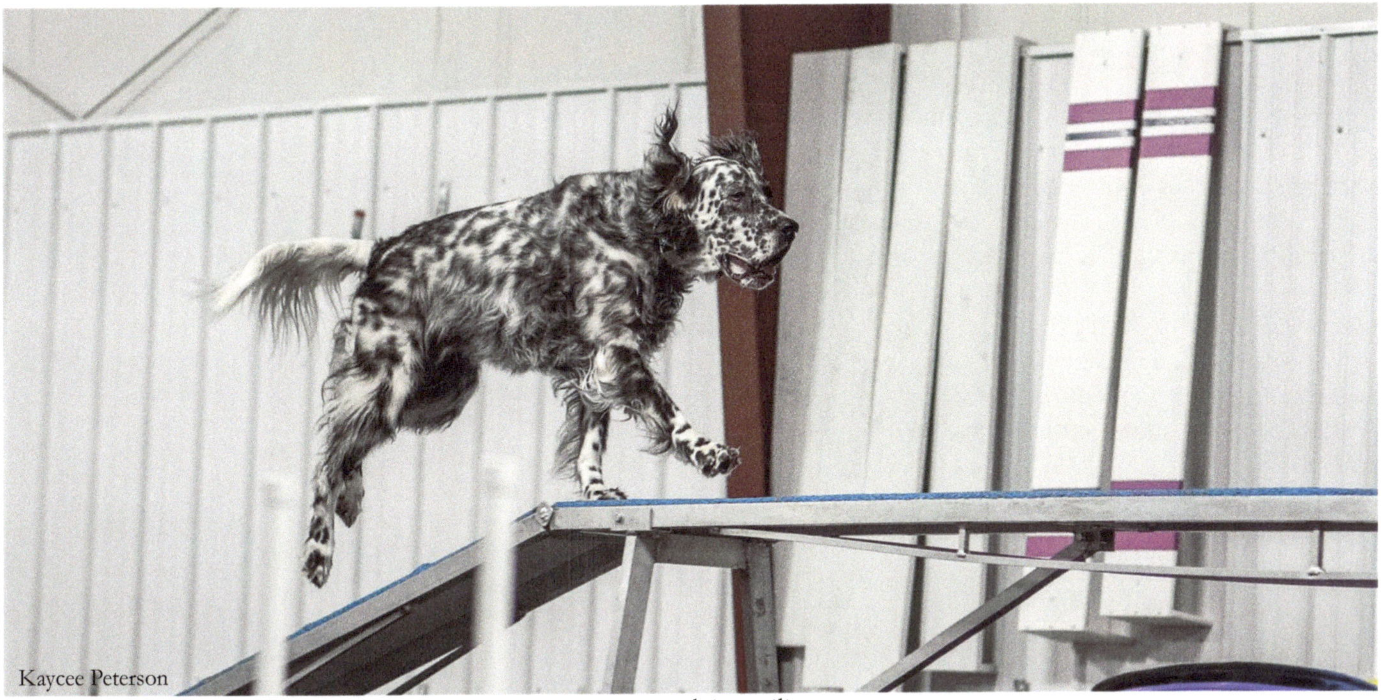

Kaycee Peterson

Kota enjoys doing agility

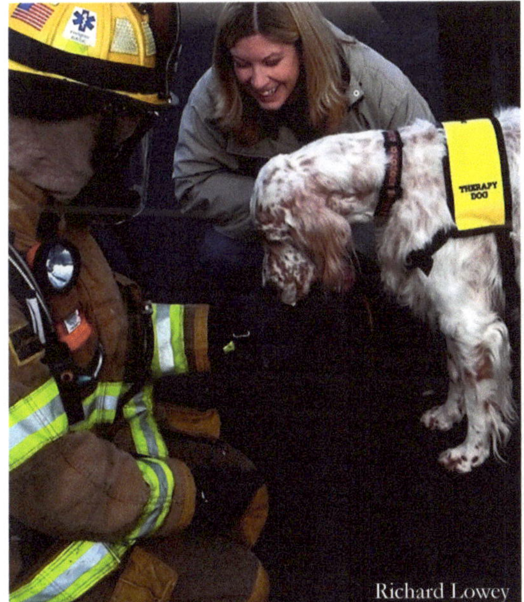
Richard Lowey

Firefighters appreciate English Setter therapy

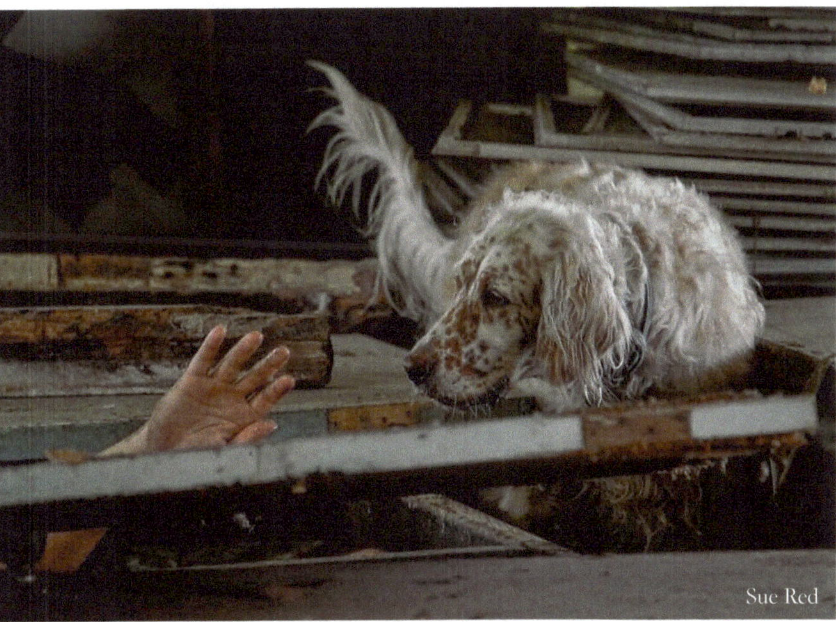
Sue Red

Zambezi locates a victim during search and rescue training

Grooming

The grooming requirements of an English Setter are going to vary with the bloodlines. The heavy-coated bench dogs will require more work than the shorter coat on a field dog. All will benefit from frequent brushing to stimulate the skin and allow natural oils to circulate. Brushing also keep tangles and mats from forming and provides some lovely one-on-one time with your dog. English Setters are prone to "Grinch feet" or "Slipper feet", fur growing wildly between toes and on the top and bottom of the paw. Keeping this trimmed up not only looks neater but will prevent the formation of ice balls in the snow and help your dog maintain traction on slippery surfaces.

Longer coated setters, such as the bench and Ryman lines, may require the occasional professional grooming to keep their coats looking trim. A "show cut" will include shaving the neck, tops of ears, neatening the line of belly fur, legs, and tail. It's generally not necessary for Llewellin and field setters.

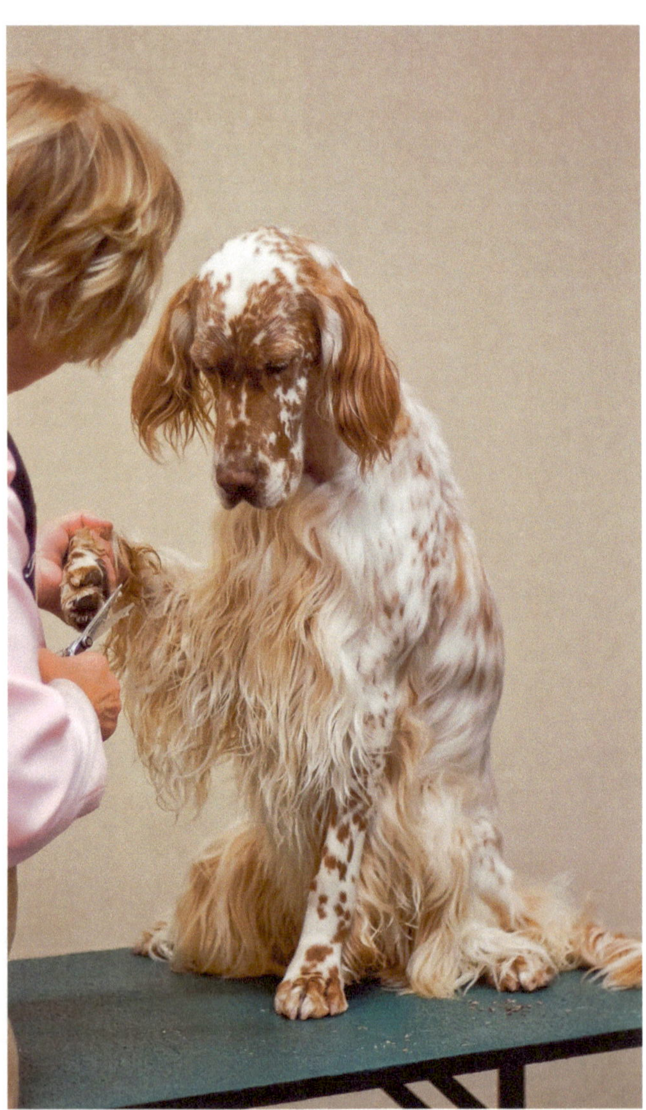

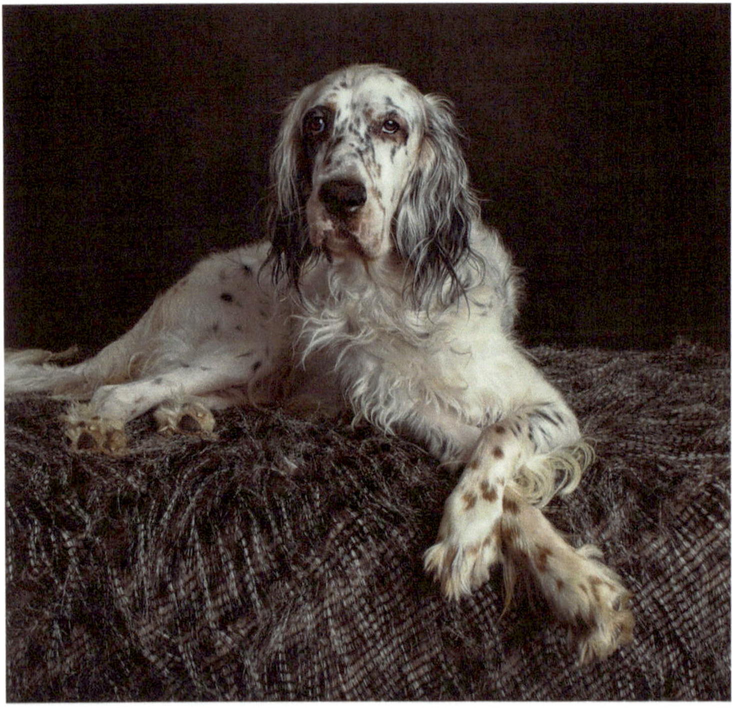

English Setters shed regularly, slightly more when the temperatures start to rise. Regular brushing will keep the fur bunnies (or fur rhinos if you're not careful!) at bay. The pale fur loves to collect in corners and around the feet of furniture and will be particularly noticeable if you have dark floors.

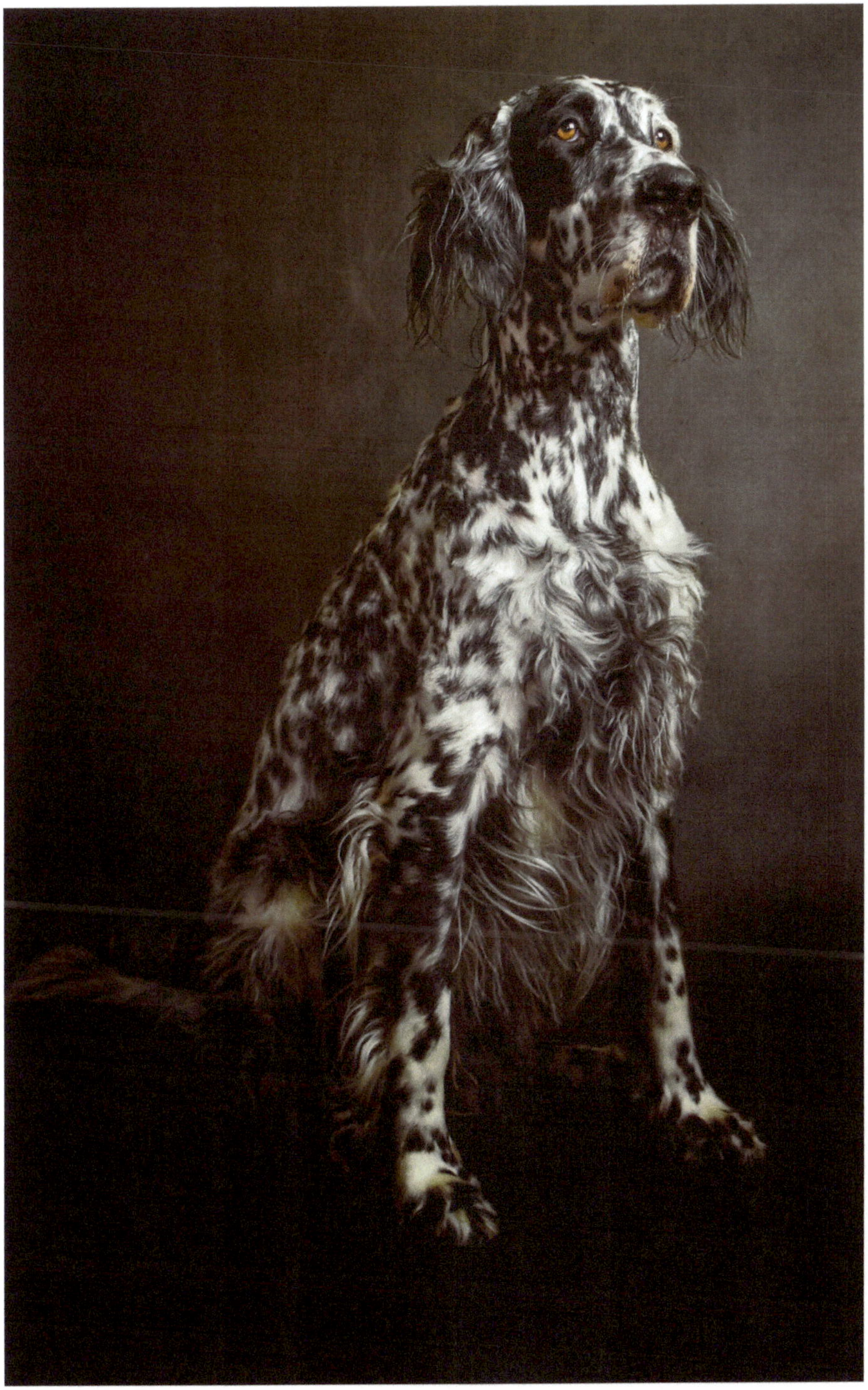

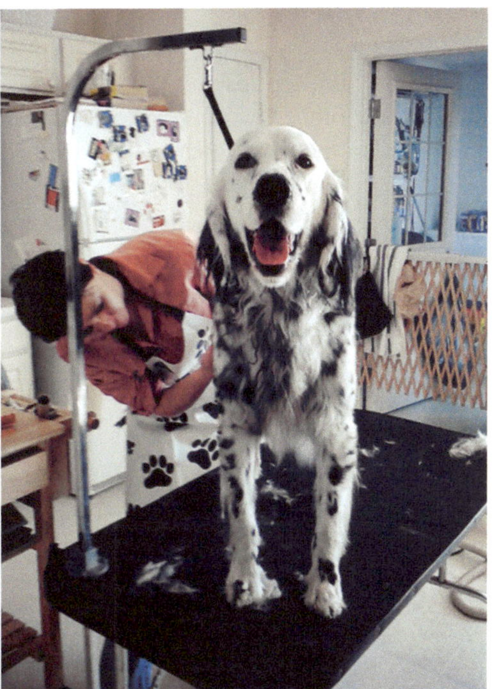

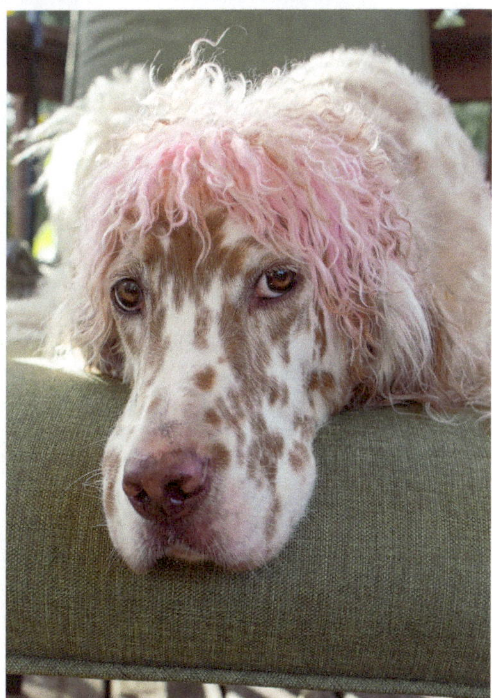

Health Issues

As with any other dog breed, the English Setter does have genetic issues. Thankfully, there are only a few. Hip and elbow dysplasia are the most common ones, with a smaller percentage suffering from allergies, hypothyroidism, and deafness. Cancer numbers are starting to increase but that appears to be true of many breeds as more toxins appear in our environments. The life span of a healthy English Setter can be 13 to 15 years.

Recent studies on dysplasia seem to indicate that although genetics can make a dog more prone to the disease, proper nutrition and exercise while a puppy is growing can have an enormous impact on the severity. If you're bringing home an English Setter puppy, make certain to do some research on proper calcium and protein levels for a new puppy and cover any slippery surfaces with non-skid rugs. Strenuous jumping and ball chasing are not recommended until your pup's joints have fully formed. If you're getting a dog from a breeder, ask to see the OFA or PennHip test results from the dog's dam and sire to get an idea if there is a history of hip issues.

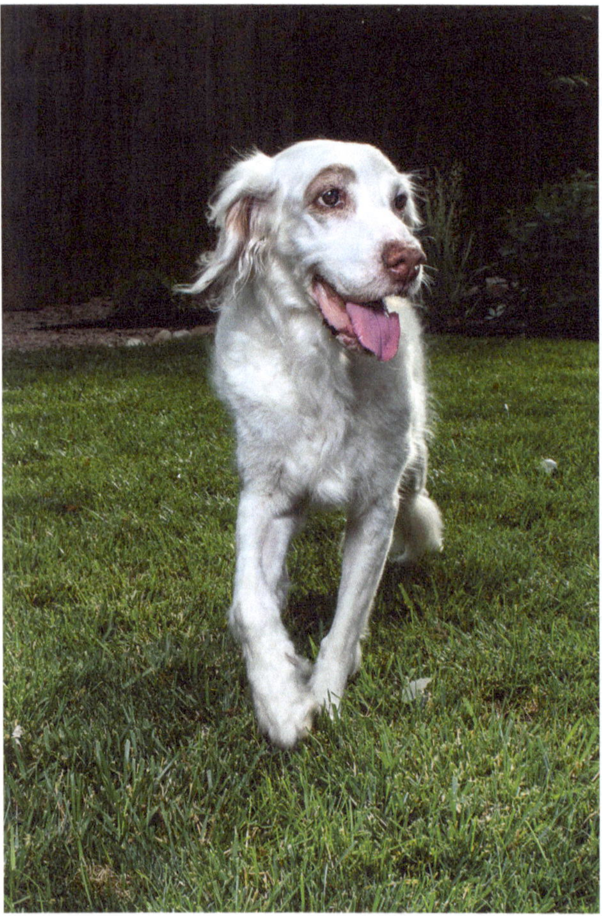

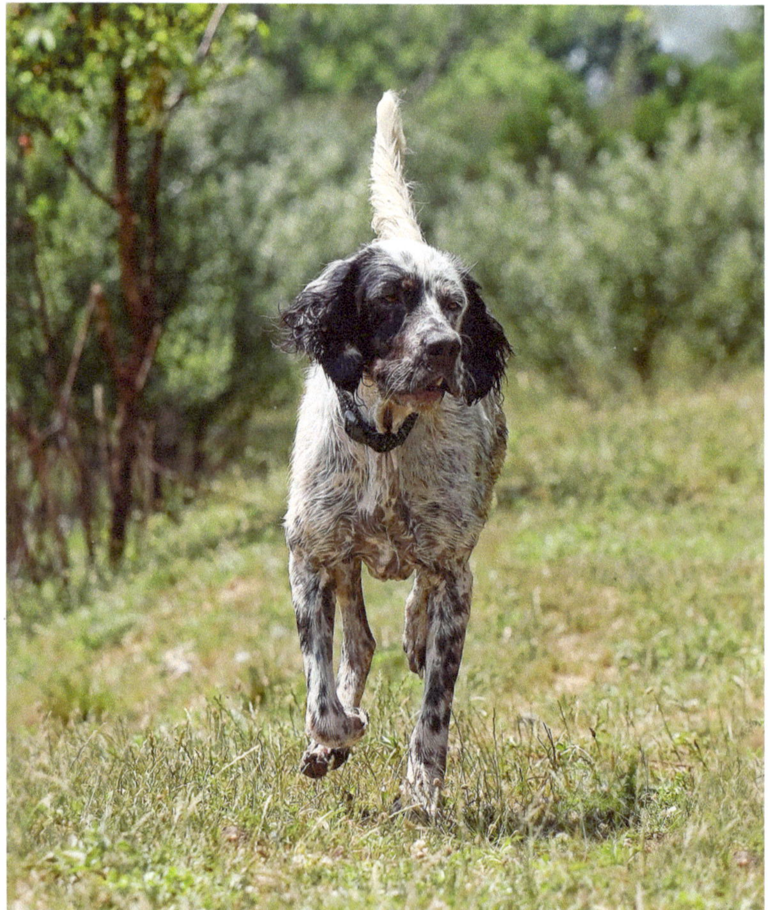

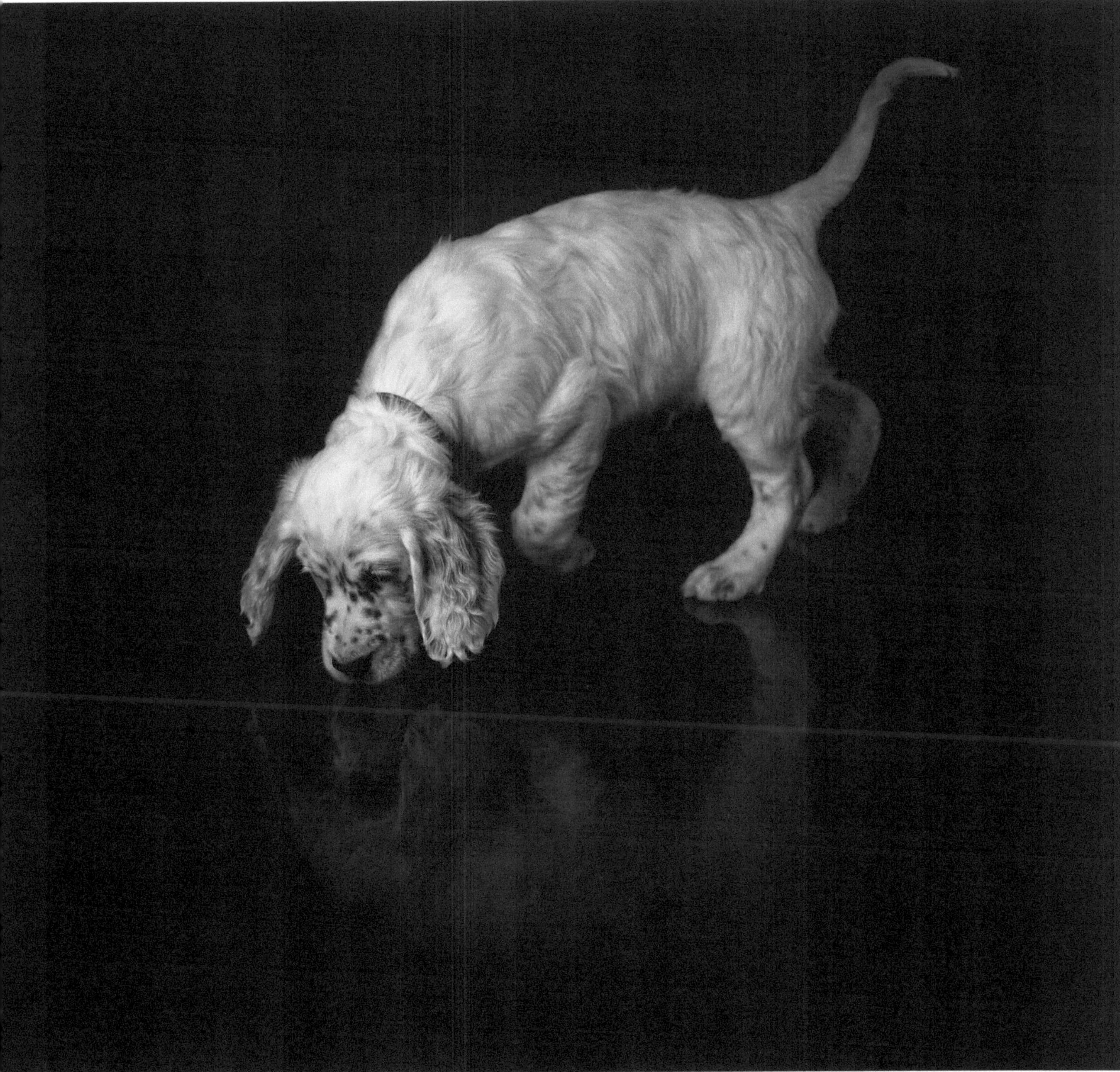

Deaf English Setters

English Setters can be born deaf. They can be hearing impaired in one ear or both and have varying degrees of deafness. Since English Setters are actively bred to be working dogs and deaf dogs are more difficult to train for hunting, some breeders will euthanize the deaf puppies. Others recognize that deaf Setters make wonderful pets and work hard to place them with the right families.

Setters that are born deaf have no idea that they have a "disability". They behave exactly as a hearing dog would. They just have a better excuse not to listen than hearing dogs! They bark, they chew on things they shouldn't, they point birds, and they climb in your lap for cuddles. Dogs communicate very well through body language and a deaf dog will quickly pick up both human and dog gestures. Deaf Setters can be easily trained to respond to hand signals instead of voice commands and hearing dogs in the same household learn to respond to the same hand signals. You should never expect less of a deaf Setter than you would a hearing Setter.

With patience and the use of a vibration collar, deaf Setters can even be taught to hunt. They have the same natural bird dog instinct – they just need to learn to respond to a different type of command. While this is usually hand signs, hunting requires that they respond to commands at a distance – thus the use of a vibrating collar (not a shock collar). Deaf Setters can also do agility, rally, obedience, scent work, and just about anything else a hearing Setter can do, including just laying around the house, looking pretty.

There are also advantages to having a deaf Setter. Imagine having your dog sleep through a ringing doorbell or a terrible thunderstorm. Deaf dogs pay no attention to the barking dog down the street and the vacuum sweeper is either ignored or treated like a toy.

Don't dismiss a deaf Setter because they can't hear. They make wonderful family pets and make you laugh and smile just as much as any hearing dog.

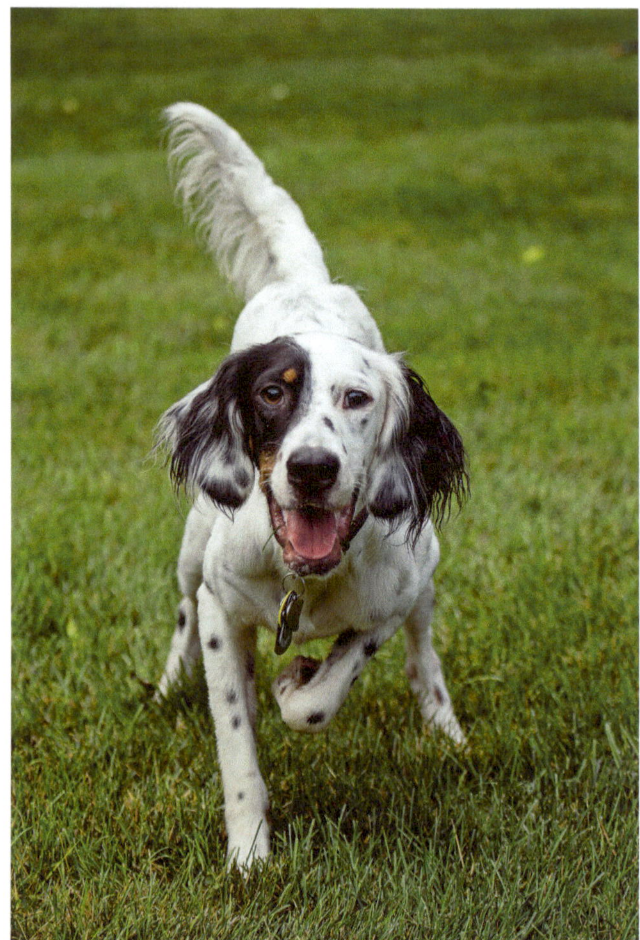

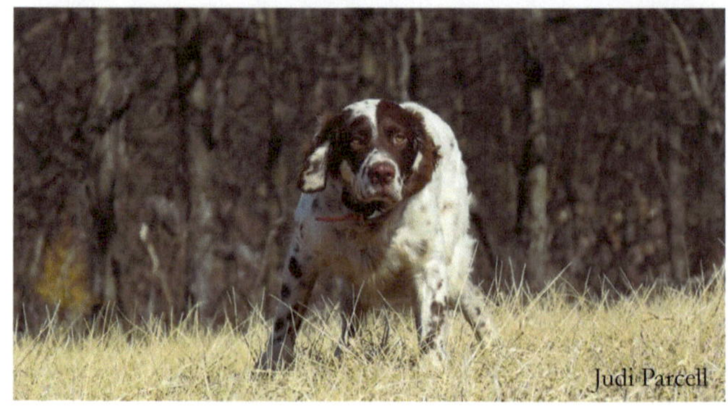

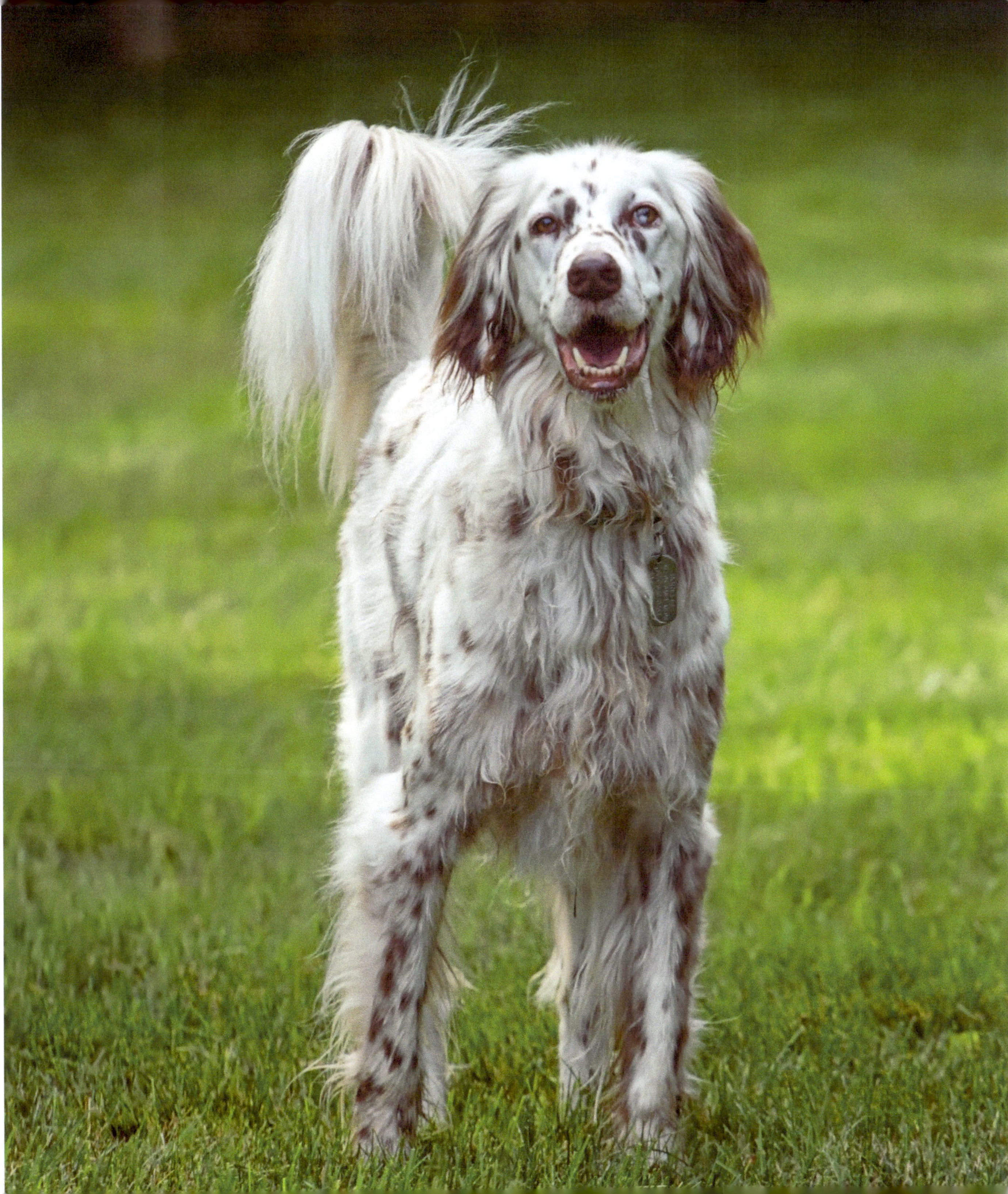

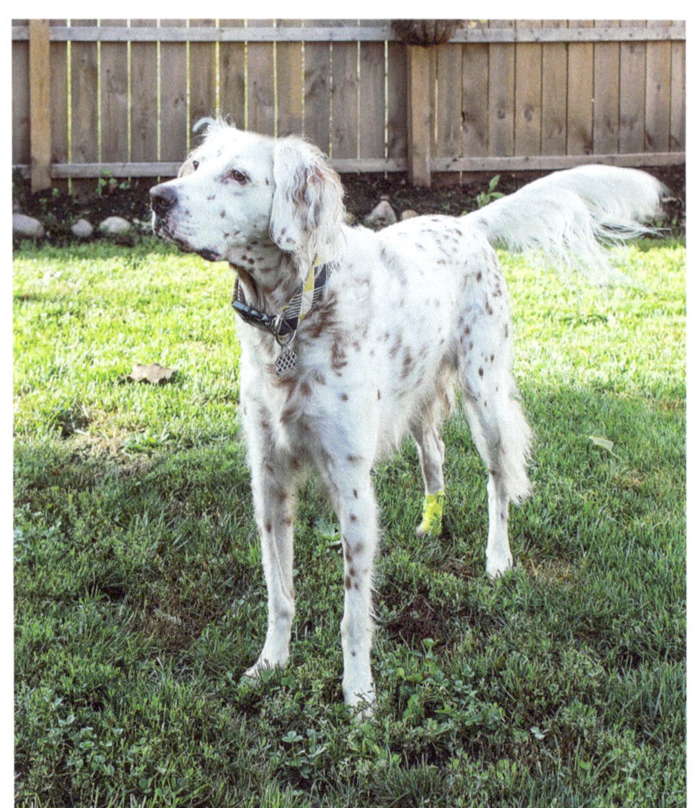
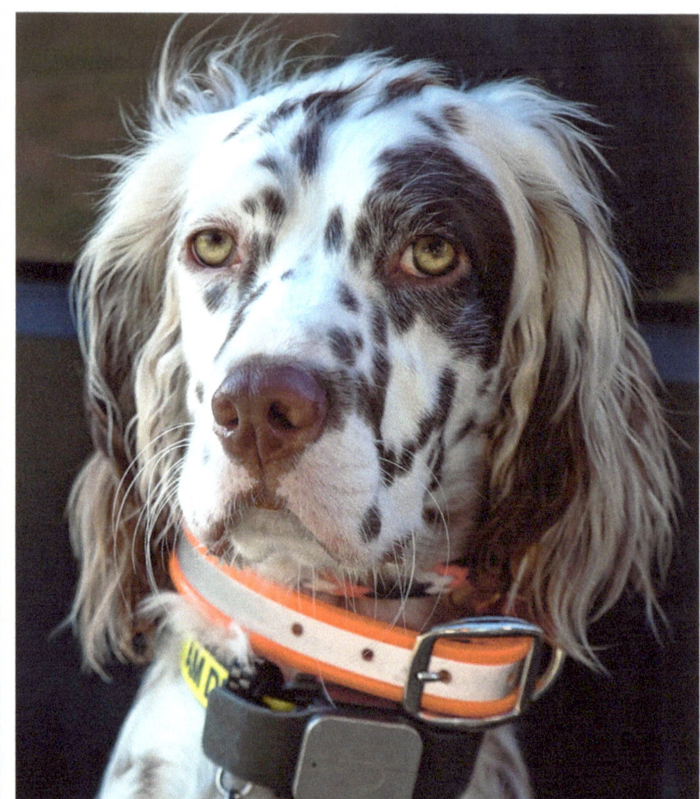

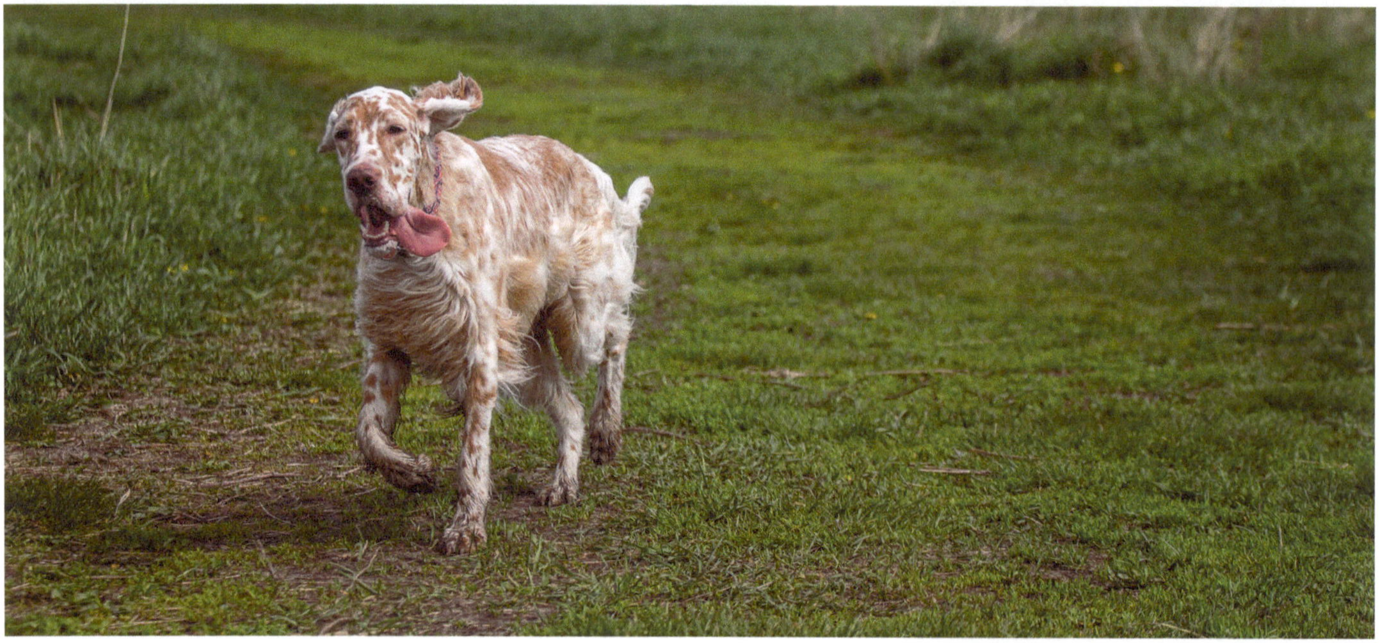

Technically, all English Setters are born with the ability to hear. The genetic anomaly that causes deafness in about 10% of the breed doesn't occur until the puppies are a few weeks old. At that time, something triggers the hair cells attached to the cochlear nerve that respond to sound to start dying off. Although the reason why isn't certain, it seems to be related to a lack of blood supply in the areas without any pigment. The pigment cells help maintain potassium levels in the cochlear necessary for proper function. To put it simply, if there's no color in the blood vessels, the potassium levels drop, the hair cells die, and that area of the inner ear no longer responds to sound.

The hair cell damage can affect either one ear or both and in various percentages. Unilaterally deaf or uni's (dogs deaf in one ear) can function remarkably well in a hearing-dog world, to the point that an owner might not realize they were hearing impaired.

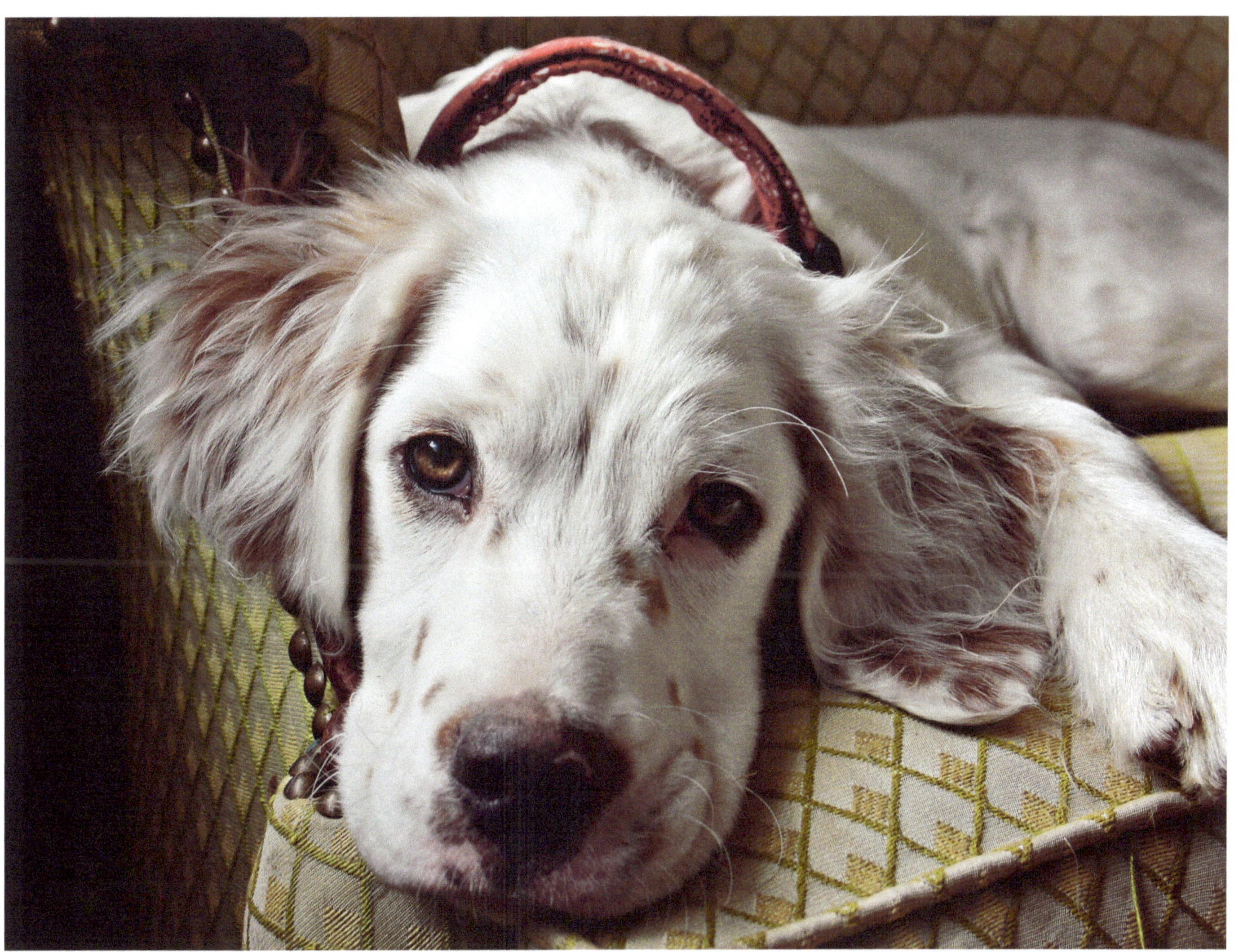

The congenital defect for deafness is closely bound to the piebald gene that gives English Setters their beautiful spots. It is not associated with any other physical defects, unlike the merle gene in other particolor breeds that also have a problem with deafness. Although deaf English Setters make wonderful pets and live full and wonderful lives, they should never be bred and the breeding lines that produce deaf puppies should be closely examined by someone with an understanding of autosomal recessive and dominant genetic patterns.

Using coat color to determine whether an English Setter is more or less likely to produce deaf pups is not statistically useful. You can also not tell if a dog is deaf by looking in their ears. The cochlear is small and deep inside the ear and even a tiny area of depigmentation could cause deafness in a dog with the damaged gene. There are all white English Setters who hear just fine and English Setters with a lot of color who are deaf.

All English Setter litters should have a Brainstem Auditory Evoked Response (BAER) test at about six weeks to check for hearing loss. The test is painless and a high level exam can be completed without anesthesia. Most university veterinary hospitals can perform a BAER test.

A recent survey of deaf English Setter owners showed that the overwhelming majority would not hesitate to own another deafie. Most of the owners also had hearing dogs in their households and were a little more reluctant to have a single deaf dog. That's because deaf dogs are remarkably attuned to their hearing pack and use them to respond to auditory stimuli that they miss. For instance, if a deaf dog is out in the yard and you call your hearing dog to come in, the deaf one will invariably follow or at least look at you so that you can give them a visual command. The main concerns to owning a deaf dog were around distance control, loud barking, and OCD behaviors. Deaf dogs, especially visually oriented hunting dogs like English Setters, are prone to nervous OCD behaviors such as "fly snapping" and "shadow chasing". These can be managed with positive behavior modification, exercise, and in some cases, medication.

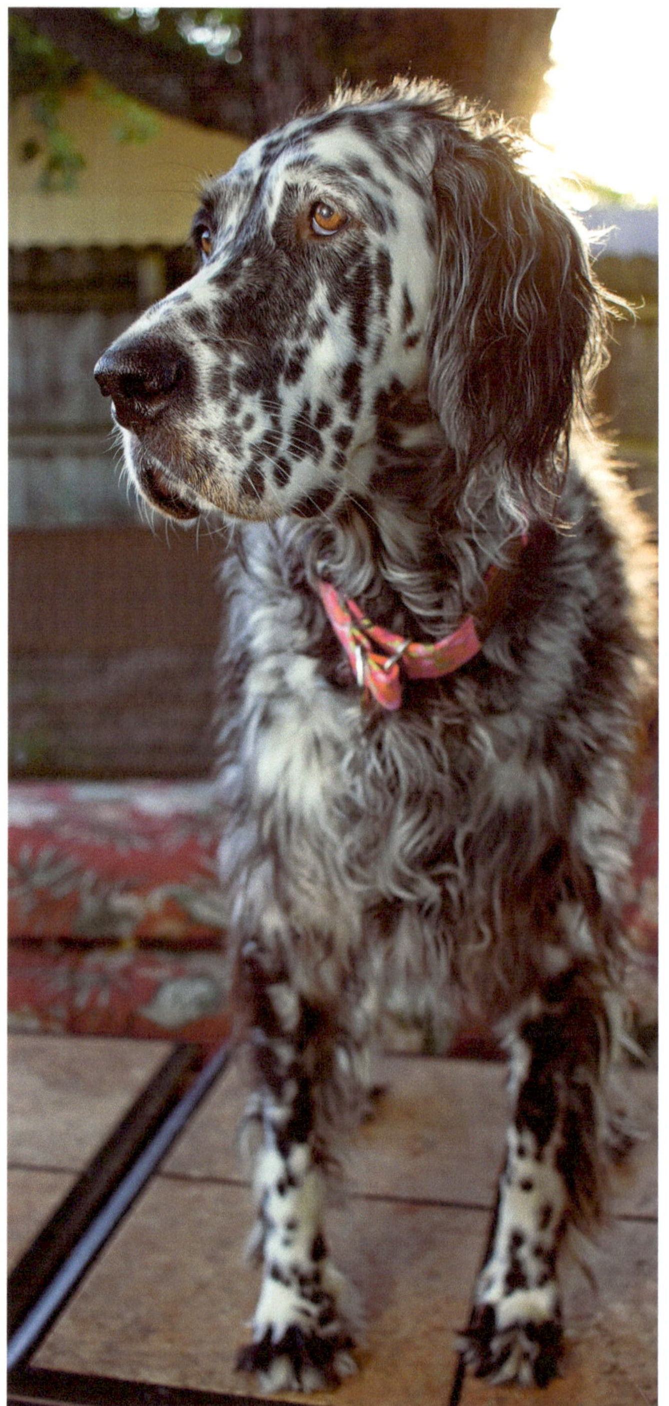

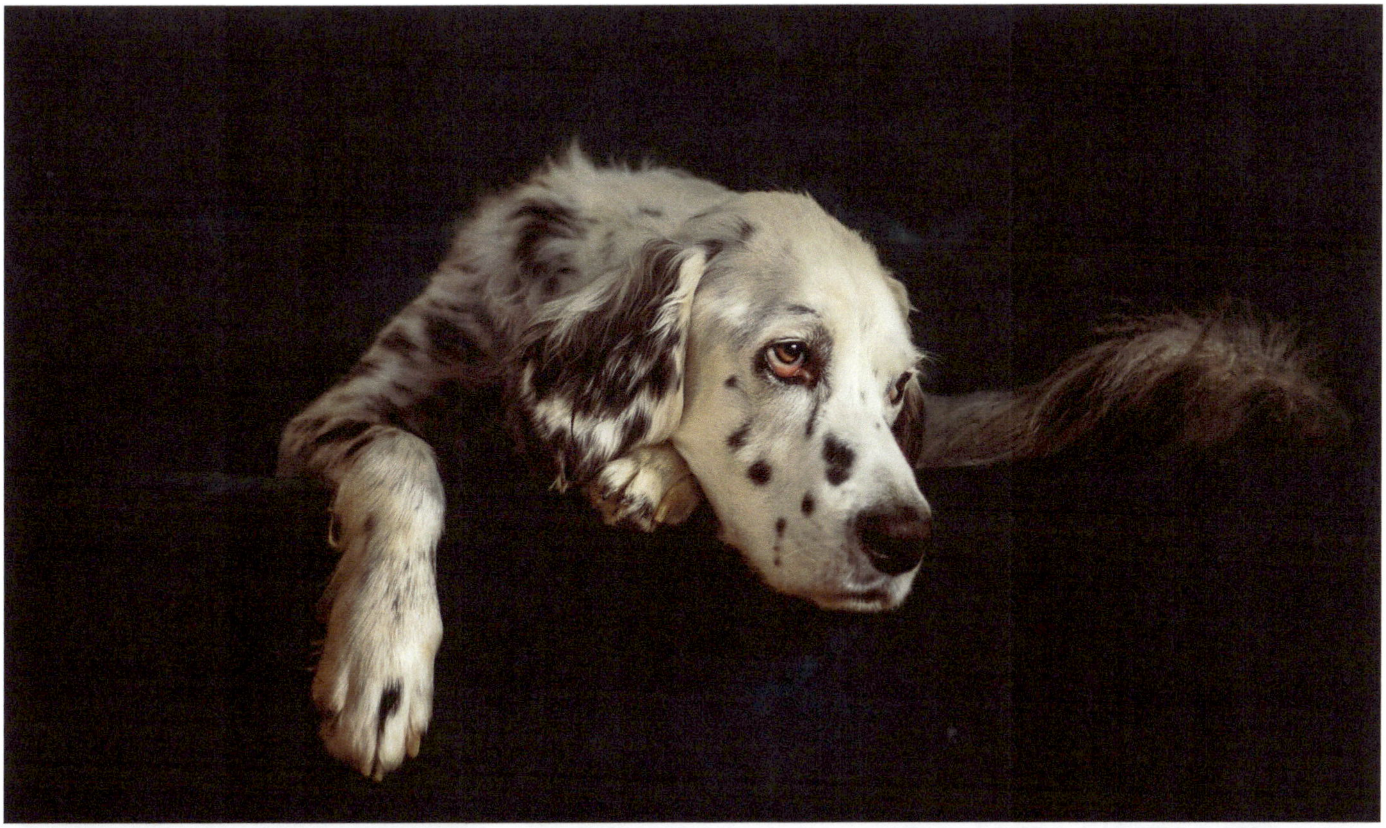

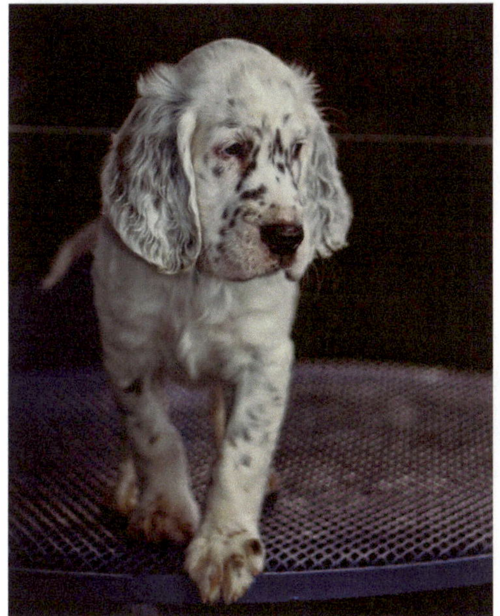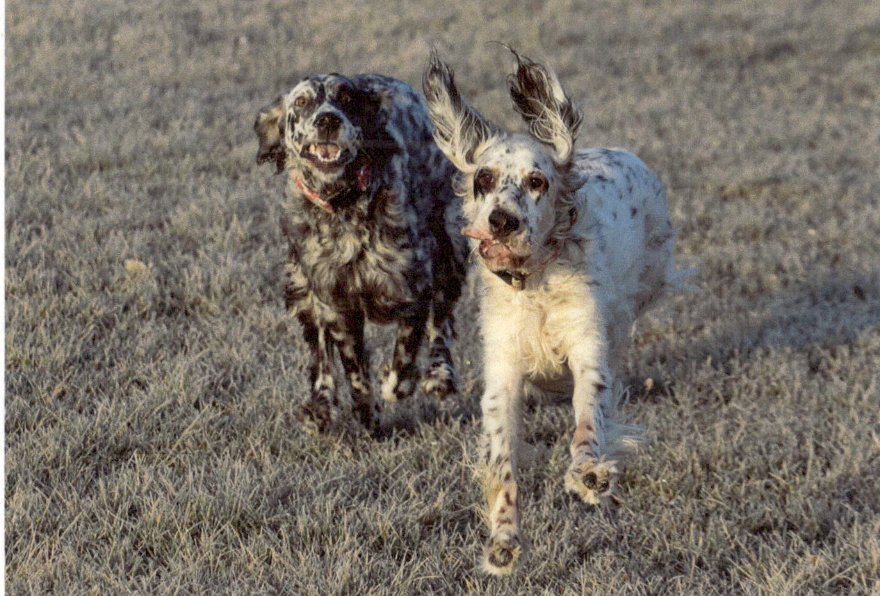

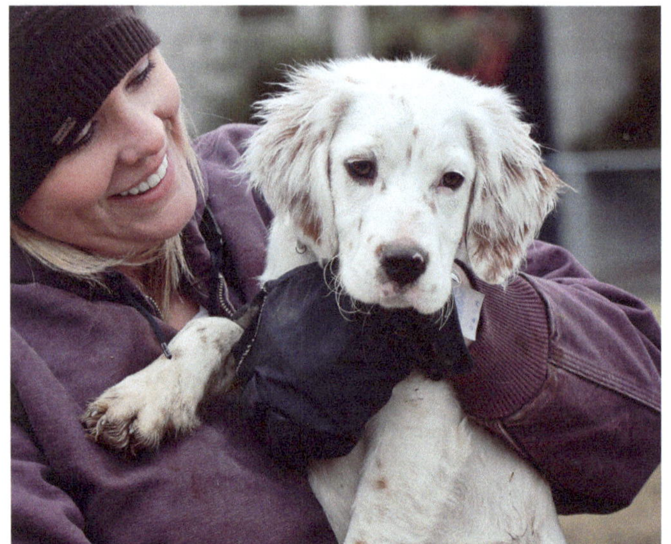

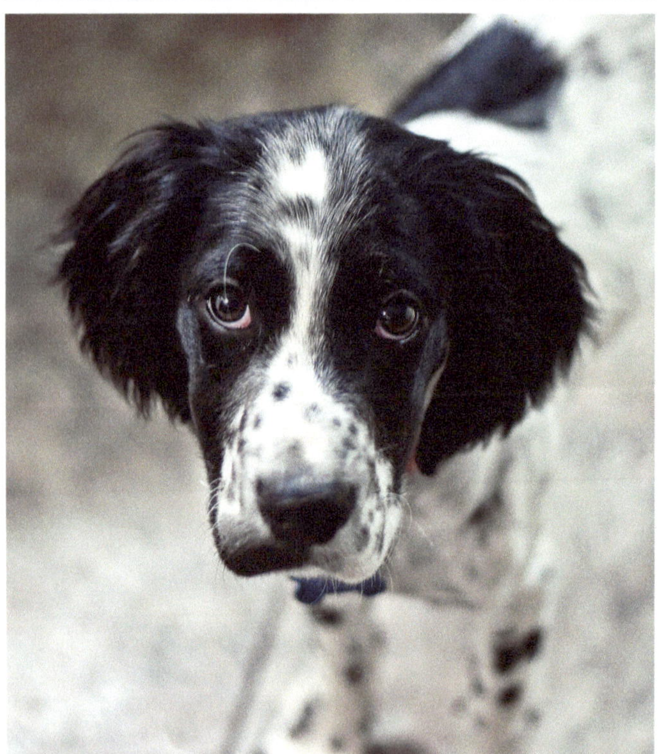

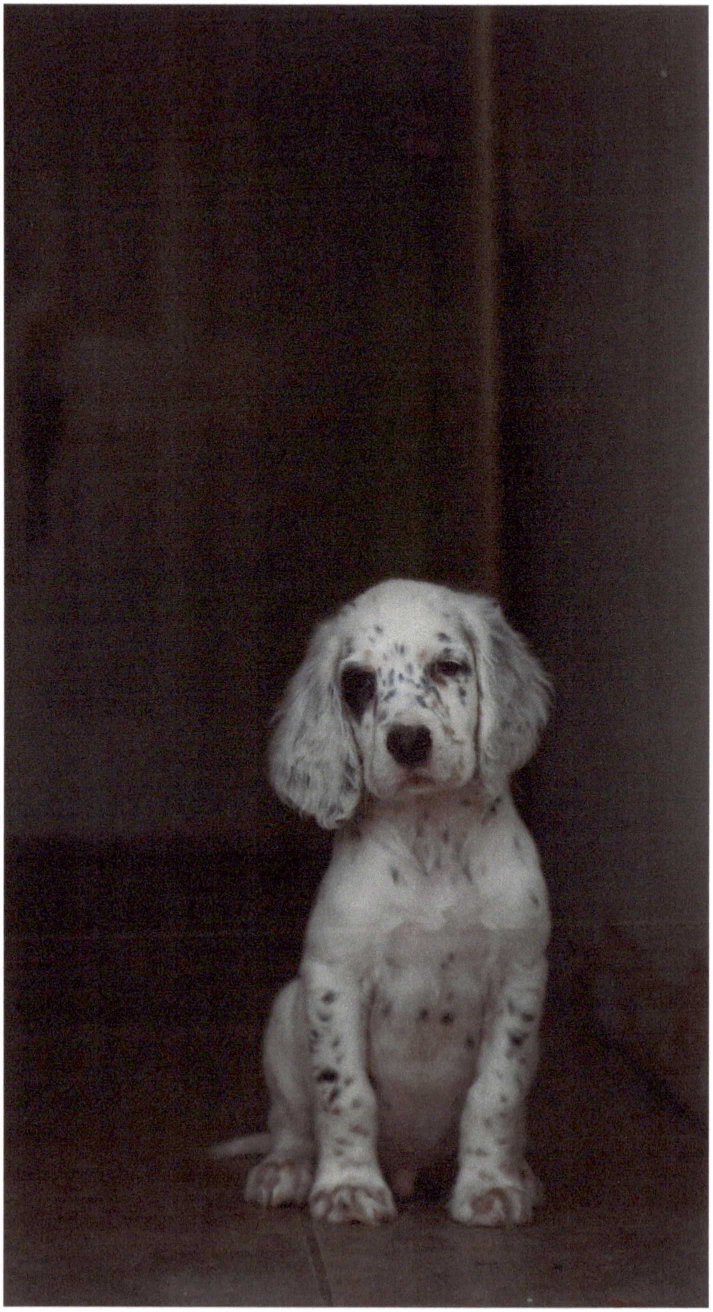

Falling in love with an English Setter puppy is very easy to do. However, choosing the right puppy is not. Even if a breed is known for a certain temperament, and litter mates may appear identical, they could develop very different personalities as they grow. Raising and training a puppy is no simple task and it will take years for the dog to fully mature. You should use both your head and your heart when you're making your choice. It's important to do as much research as possible on English Setters before deciding to bring home a rambunctious puppy as this is a life-long (for the dog) relationship that you are establishing. There are plenty of resources online and in print on evaluating puppy health and temperaments so do your homework, but expect surprises!

In addition to researching the breed, make sure you find a responsible breeder. The breeder should be knowledgeable about the breed and honest about any genetic issues that can affect them. Breeders should be willing to share proof of health screenings – for English Setters, that includes a BAER (Brainstem Auditory Evoked Response) test for hearing and OFA/PennHIP results on the sire and dam's hips. Visit the breeder's home or kennel and ask to see at least one of the puppy's parents to get an idea of what the future holds for your dog in terms of temperament and appearance. The dogs and puppies should be clean, well fed, lively, and friendly. Establish a relationship with the breeder as they can provide you with a lot of good information about your puppy as he grows. The breeder should provide you with a contract that includes provisions that they will take the dog back if there are any issues. Expect to answer a lot of questions as a responsible breeder will be very concerned about where their dog is going.

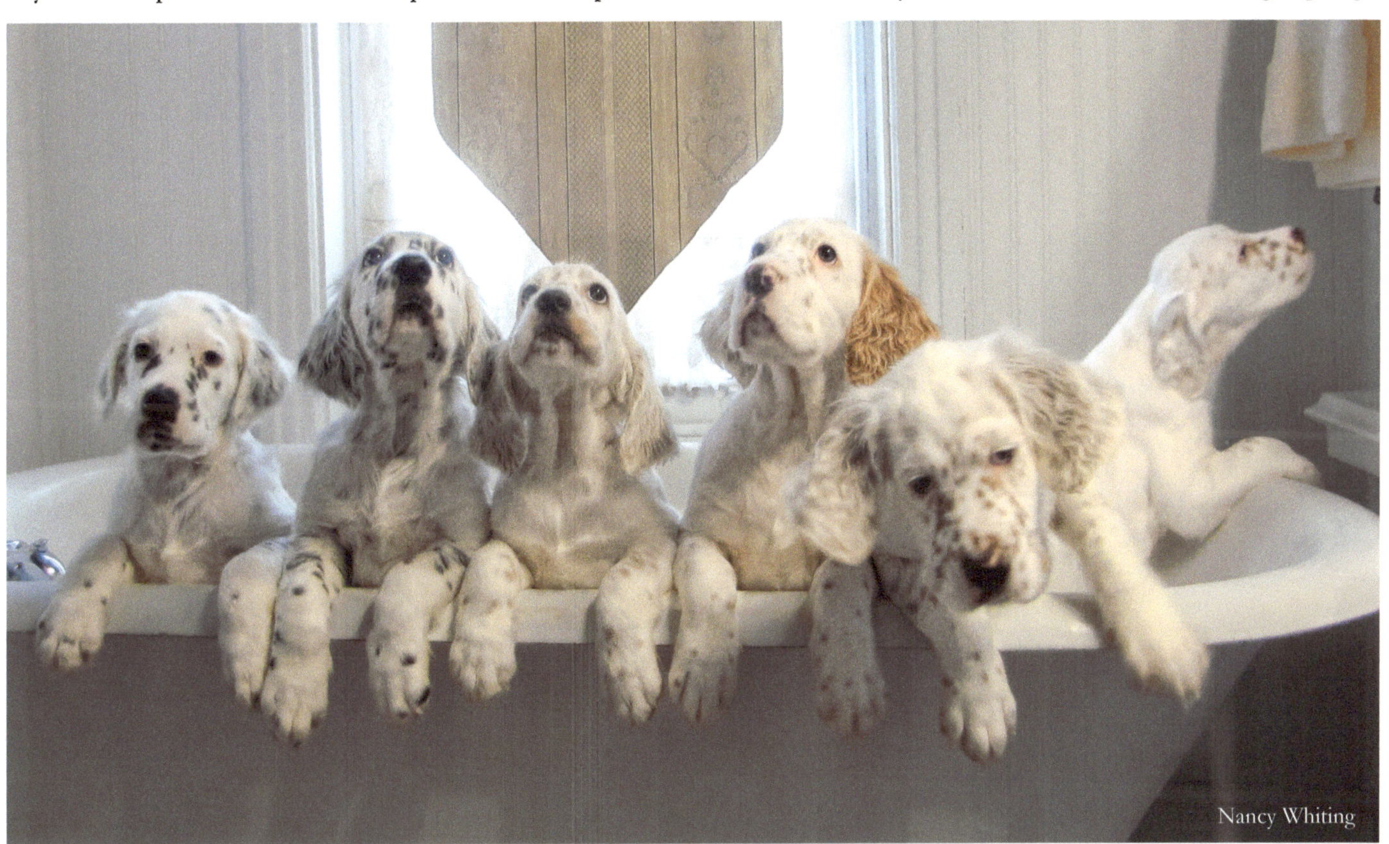

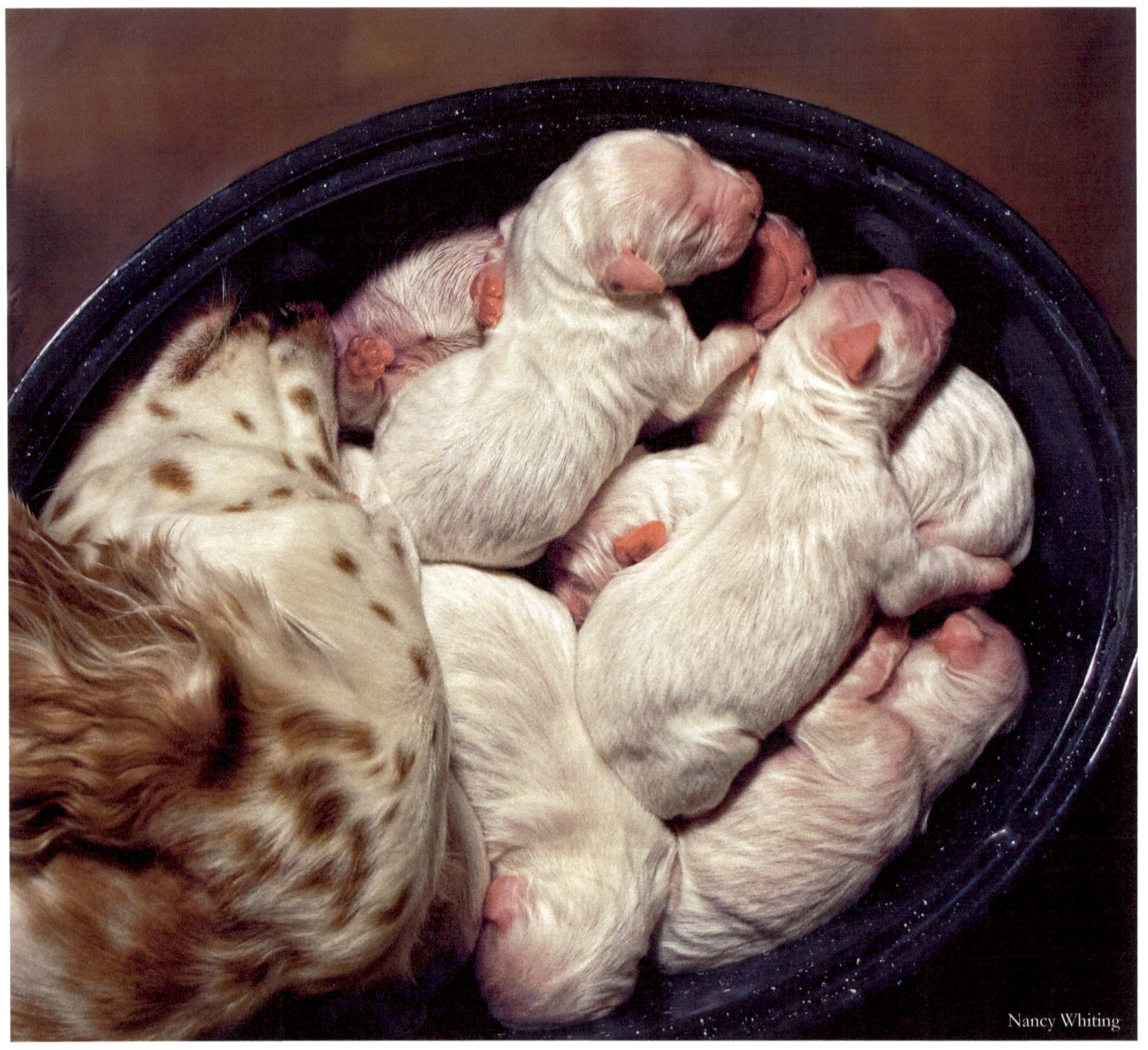

English Setter puppies are born mostly white and will develop their spots as they get older. By the time they're ready to go to new homes, between 8 to 10 weeks, the color of their spots should be apparent but their number is anybody's guess! The long flowing Setter coat takes about two years to grow in fully.

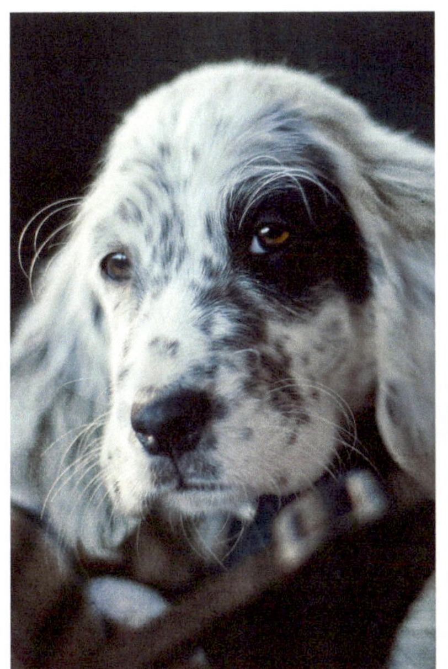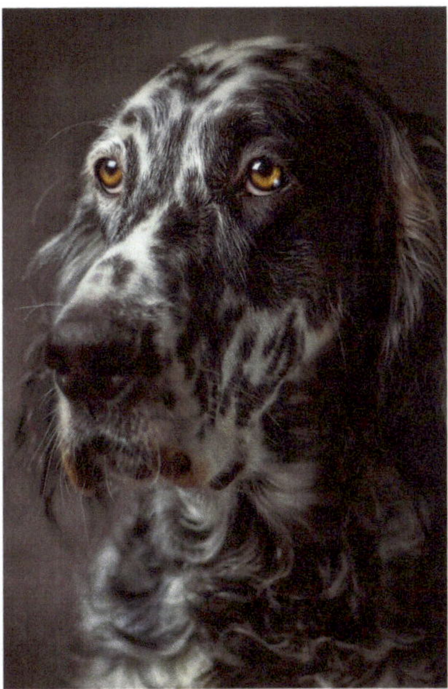

The same dog at 8 weeks and then two years

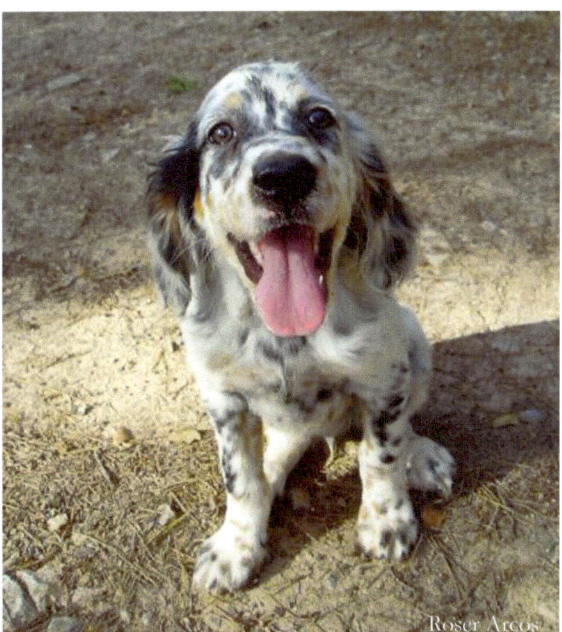

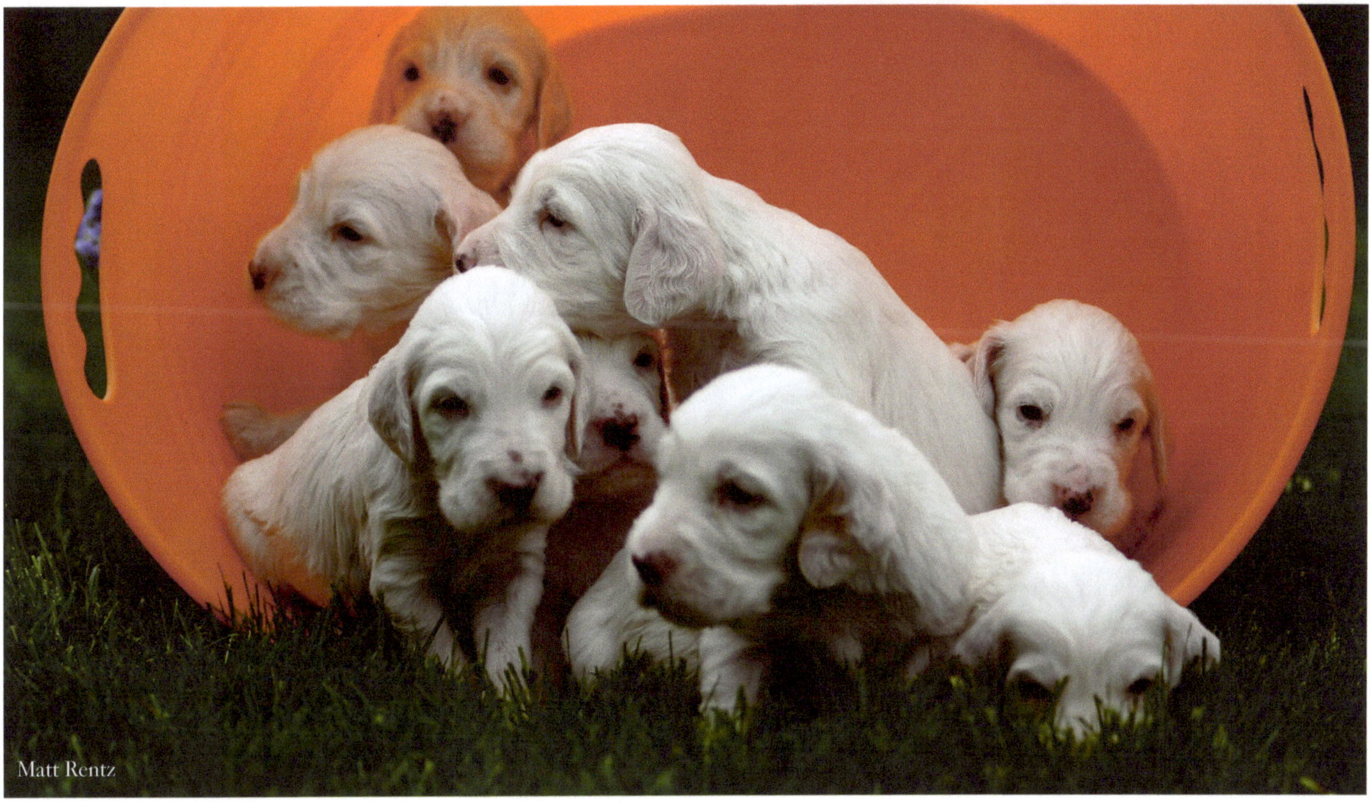

Puppy socialization and training is a very important part of building a bond between you and your new puppy. As long as it is at least seven days since your puppy has had its first set of vaccinations, it should start class as soon as possible. Starting later means missing an opportunity. When it comes to puppies, right now is the very best time to socialize, build correct habits, and identify potential problems. Puppies are constantly learning from the day they're born and are particularly responsive to retaining new experiences encountered during the first 13 to 16 weeks after birth. That means that as a new owner, it's your responsibility to assist in providing as many of these learning and socialization experiences with other dogs, children, adults, and different environments during that optimal period. Many veterinarians are now recommending that puppies should begin taking socialization classes beginning at 8 to 9 weeks of age.

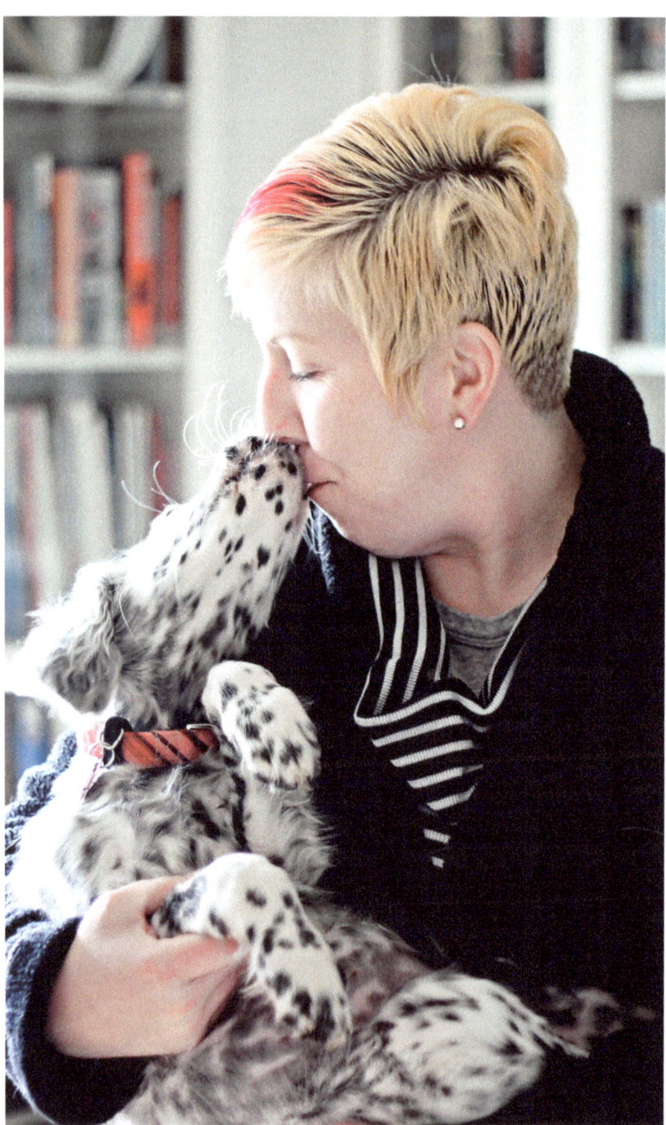
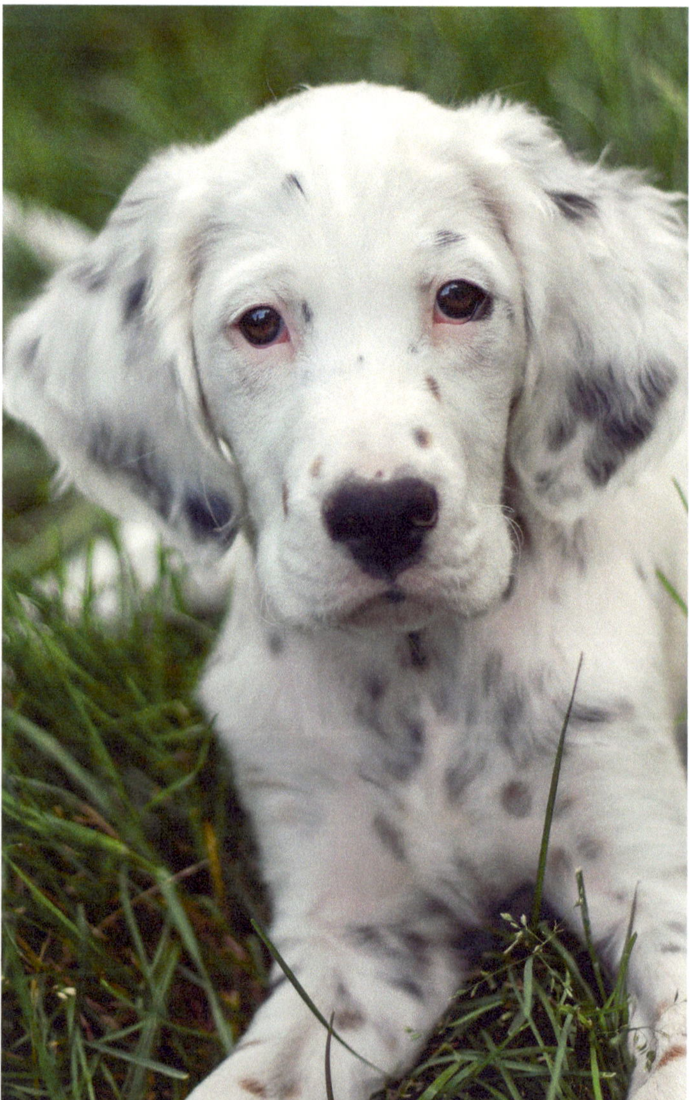

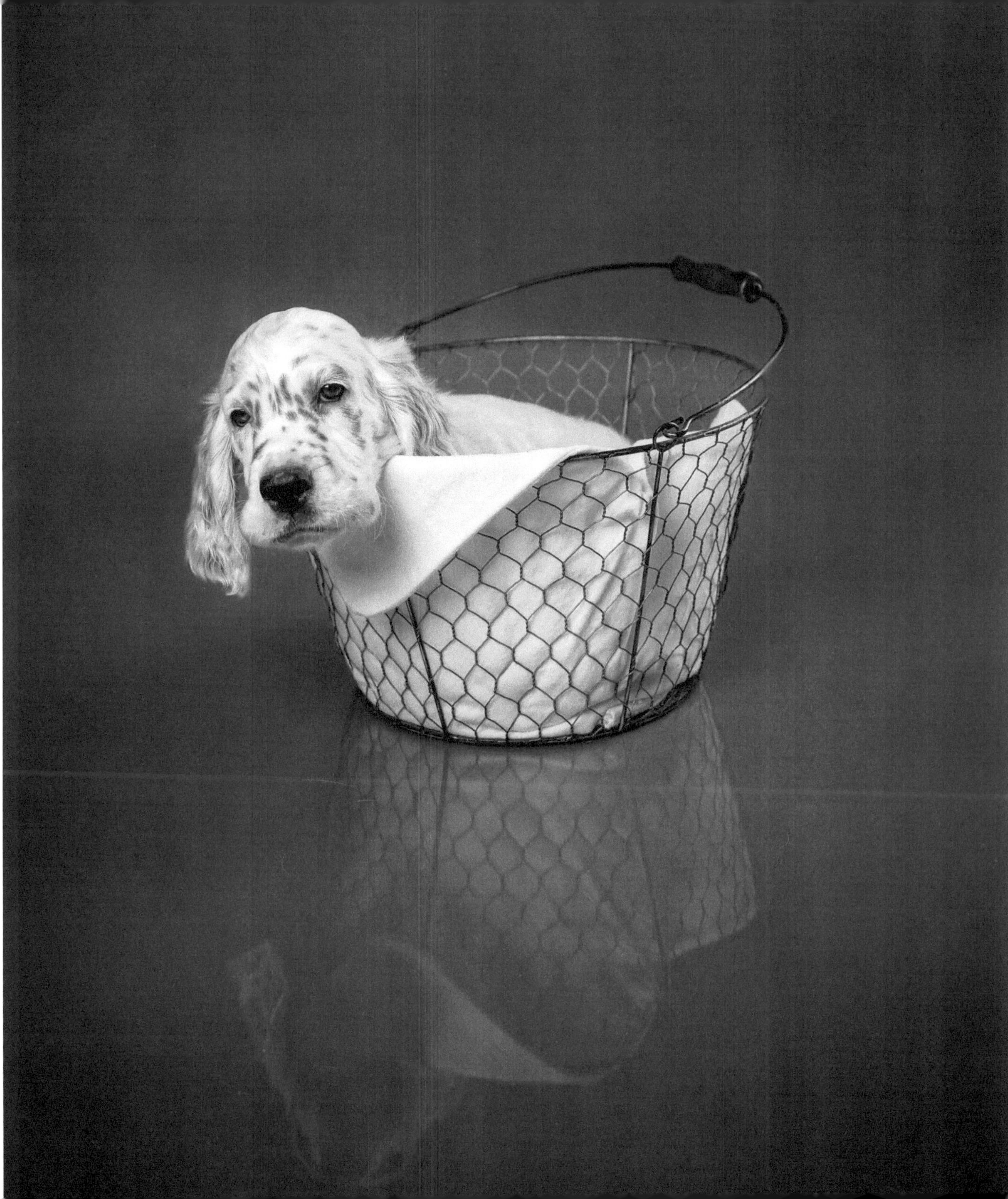

Roser Arcos

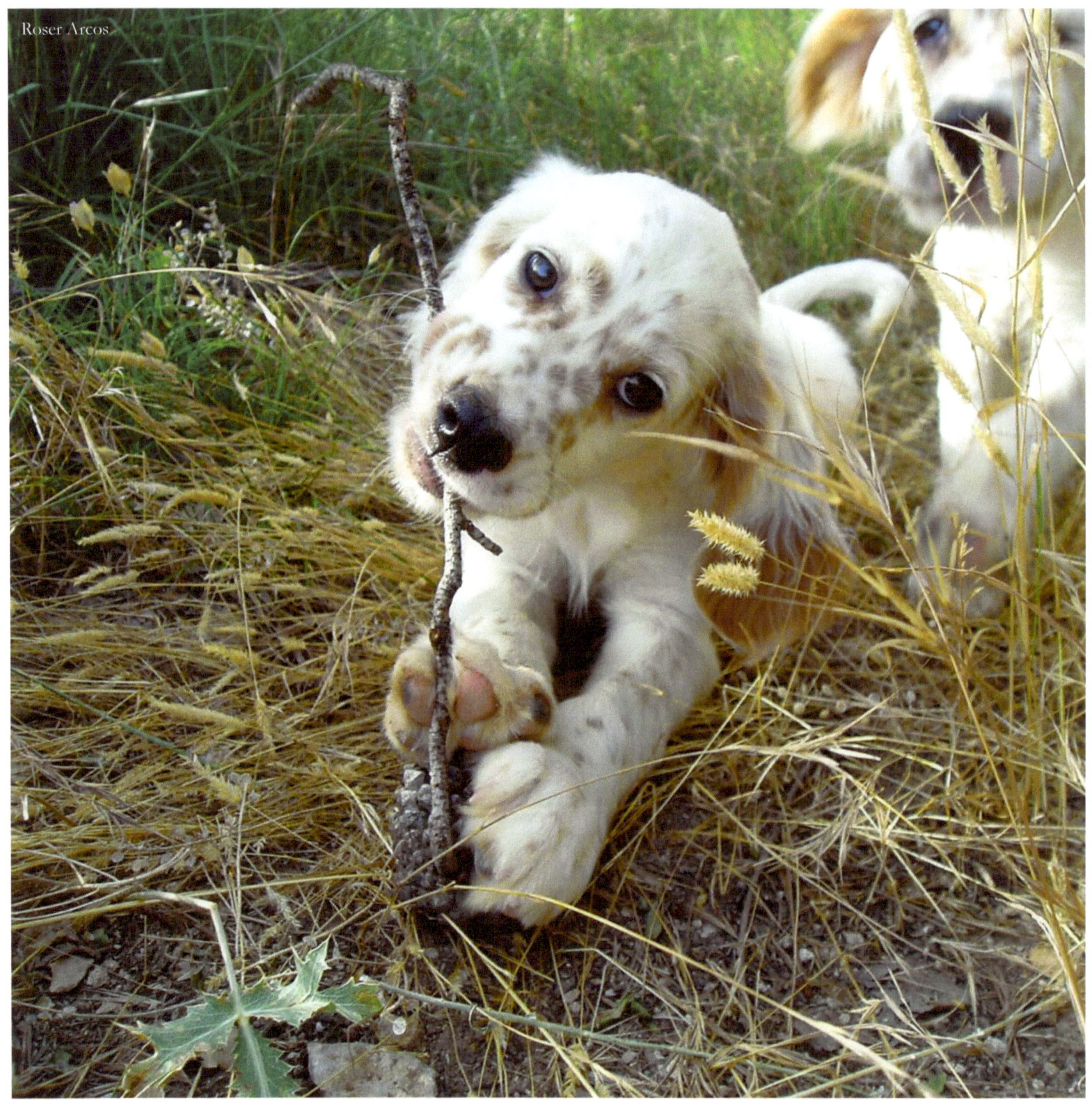

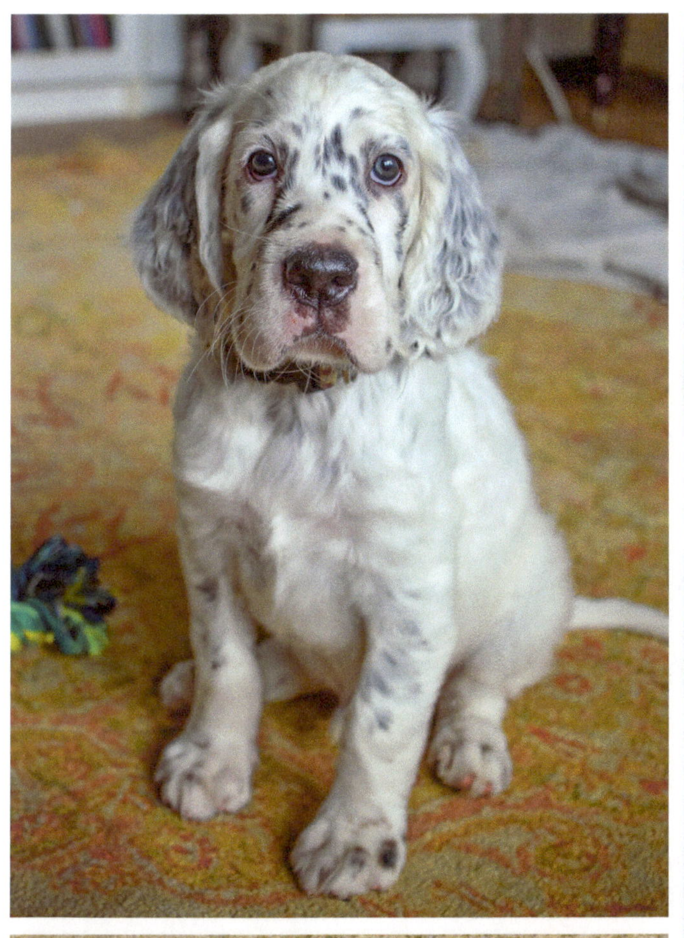
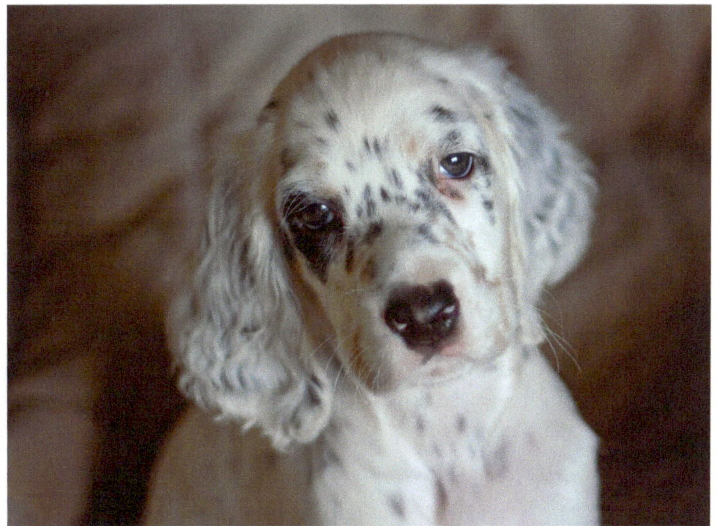
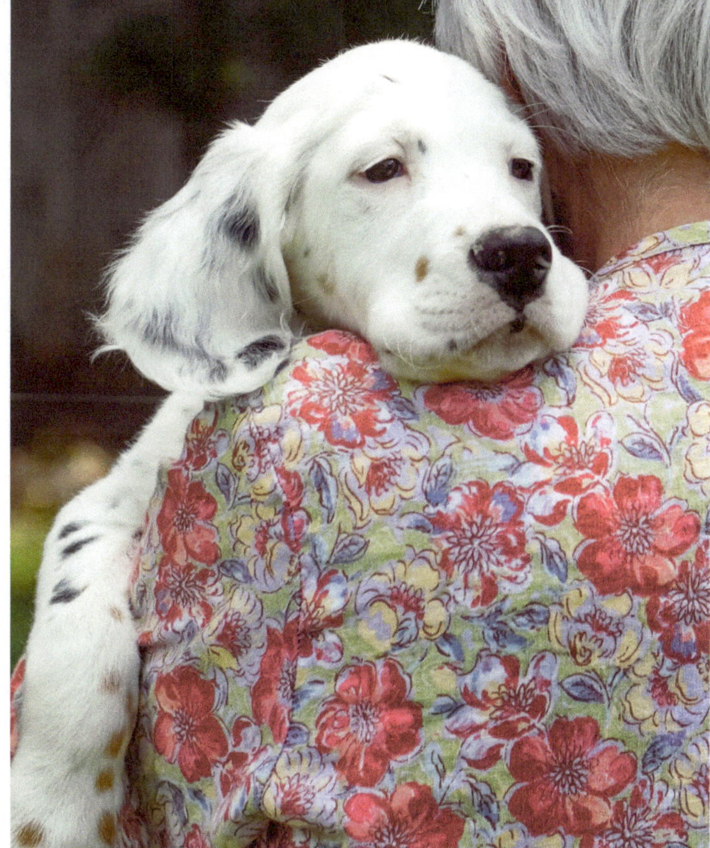
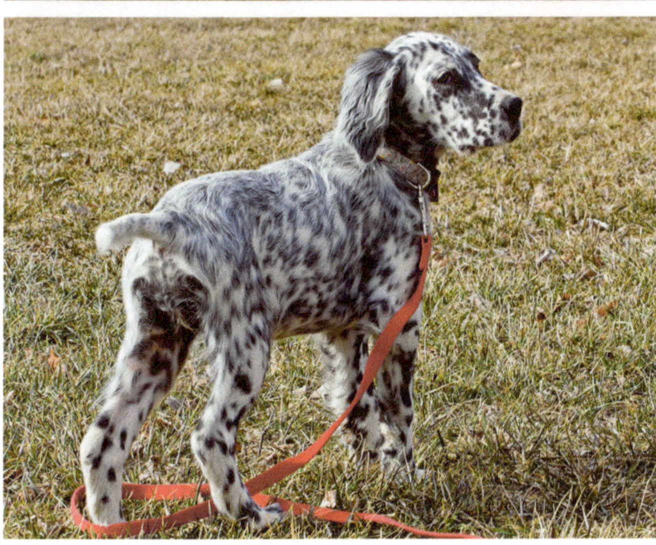

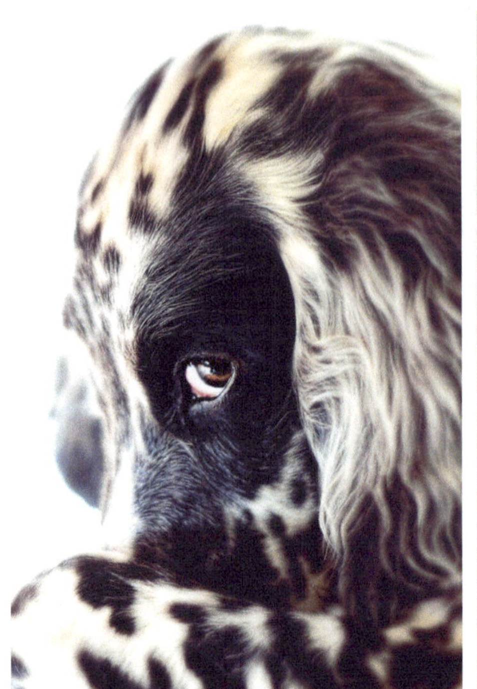

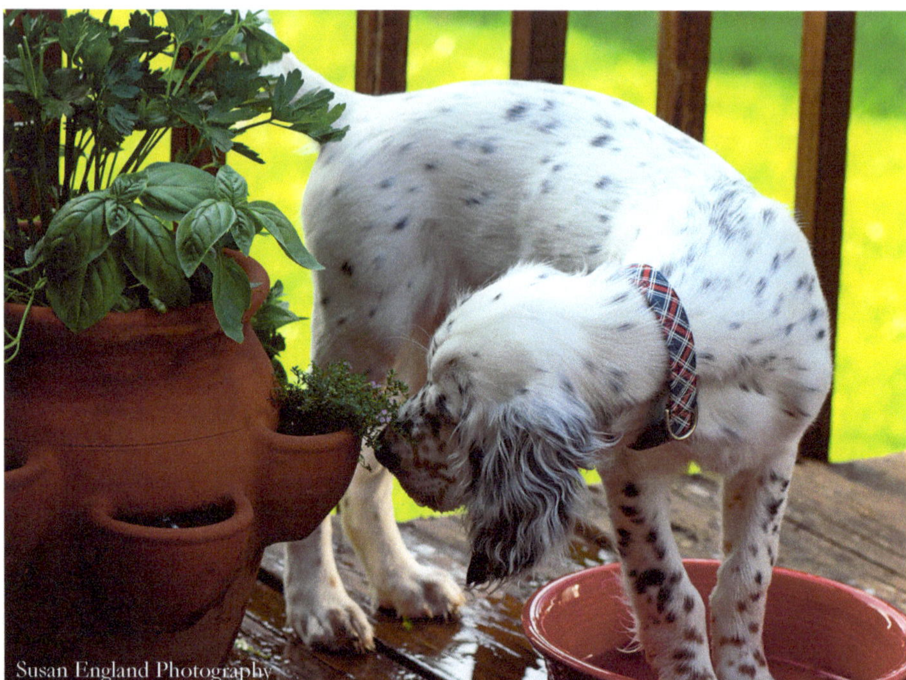
Susan England Photography

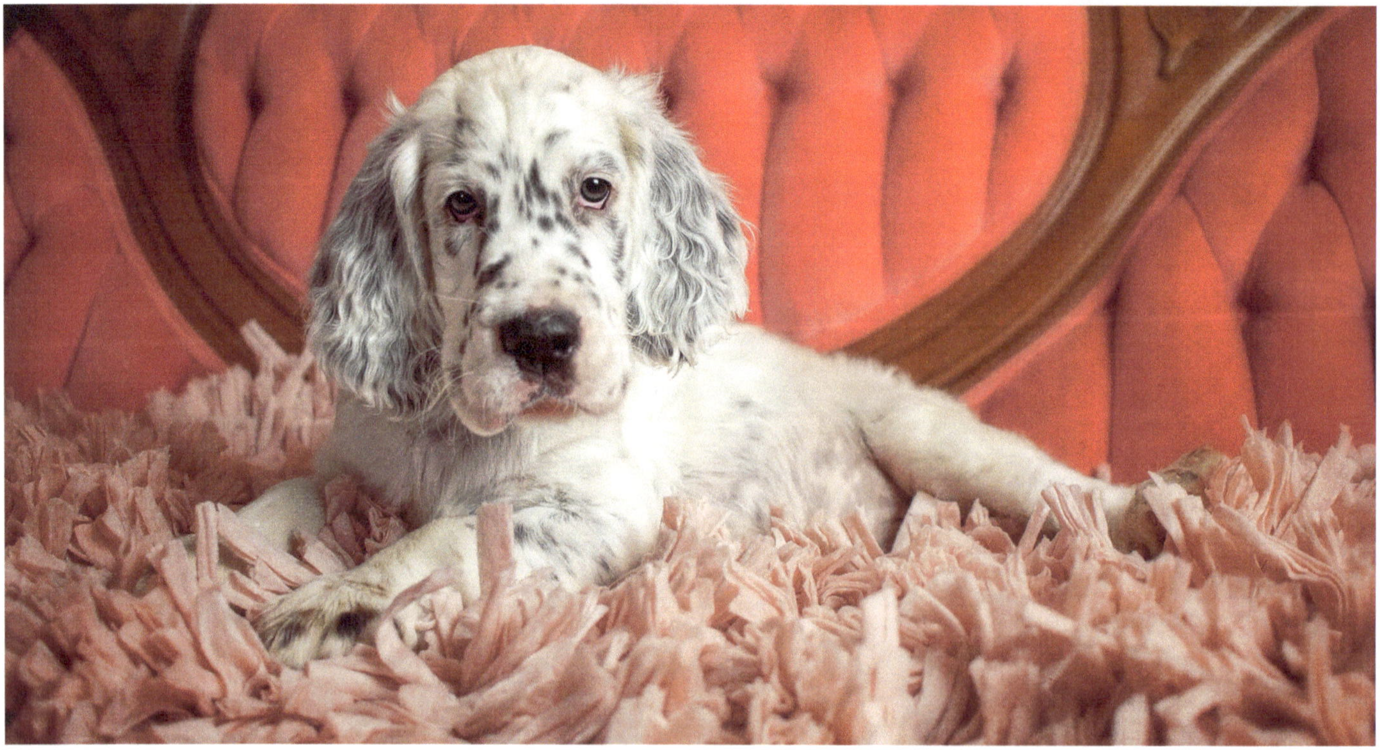

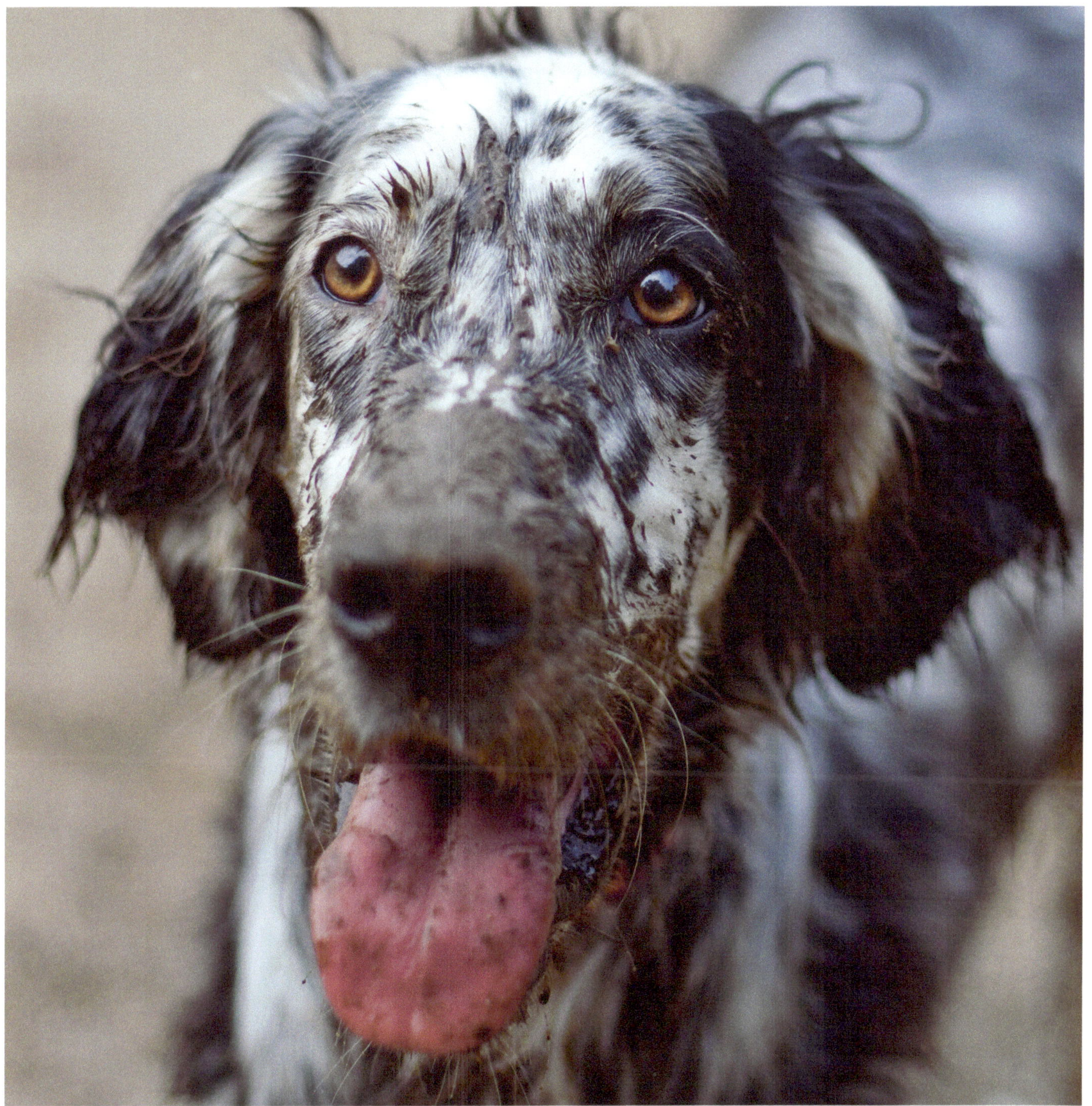

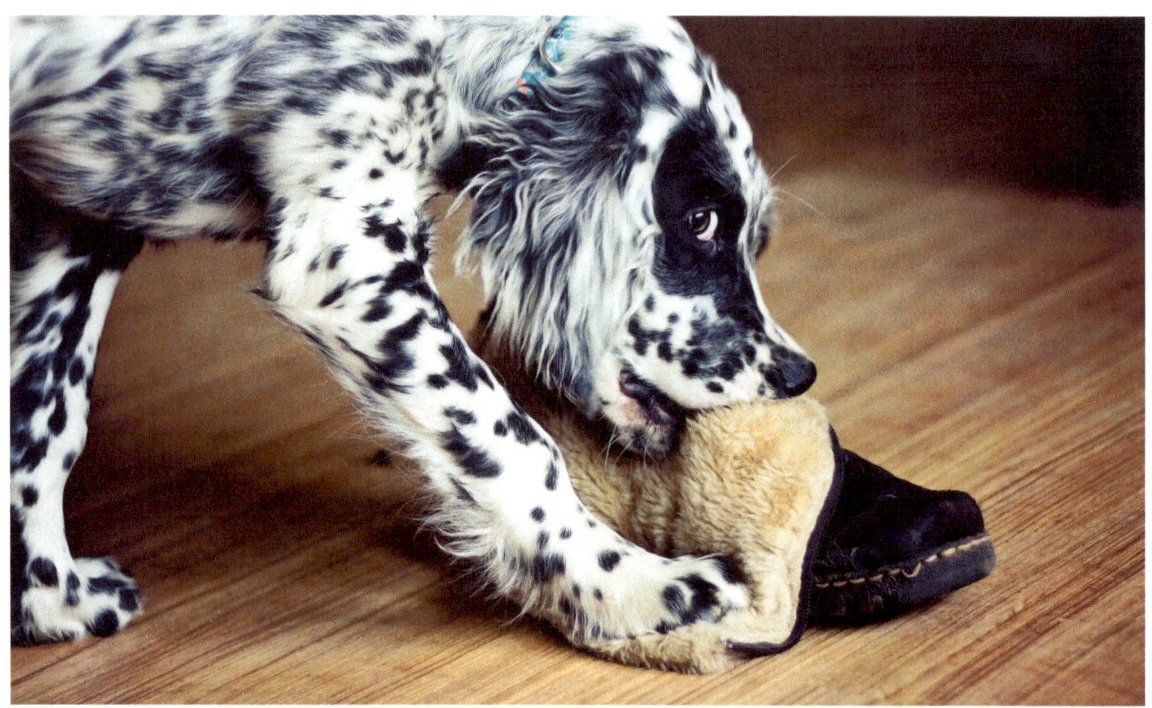

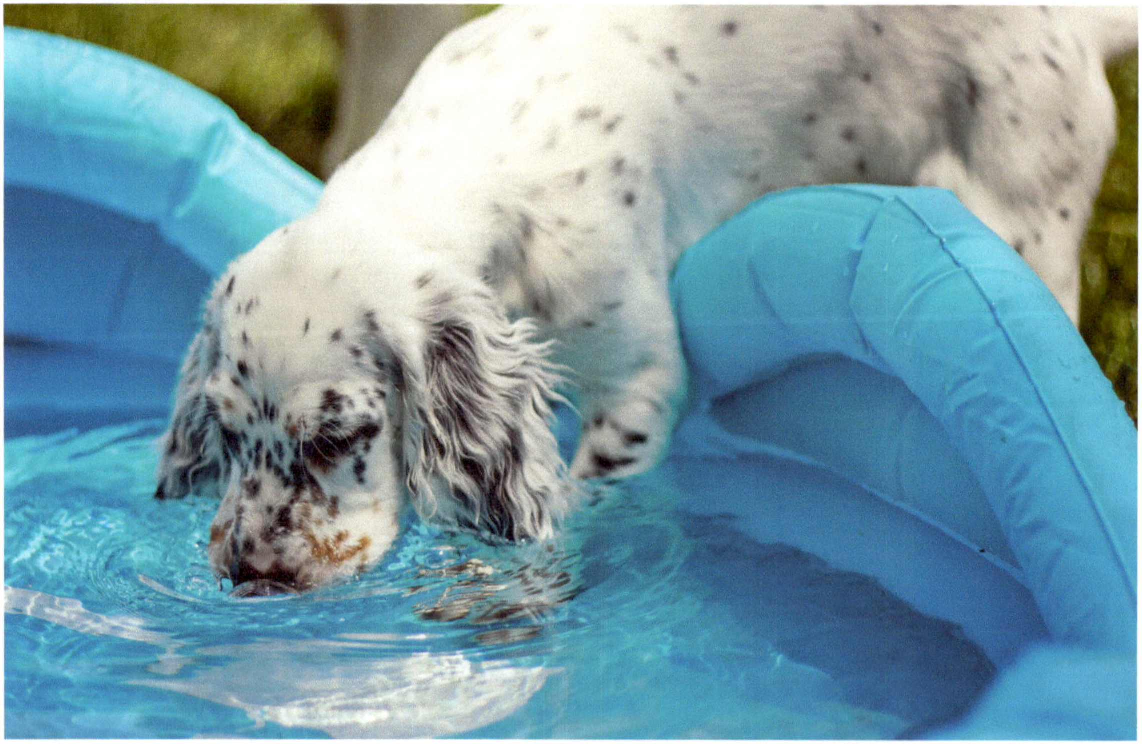

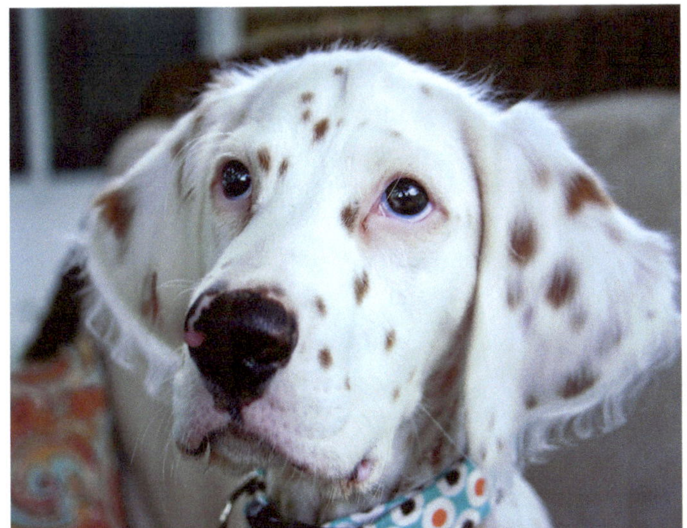
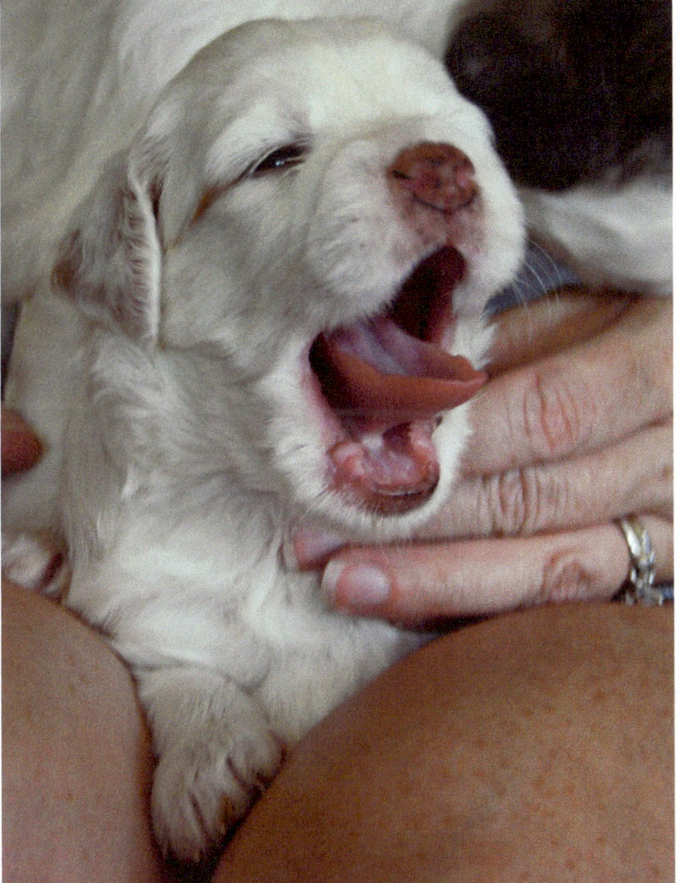
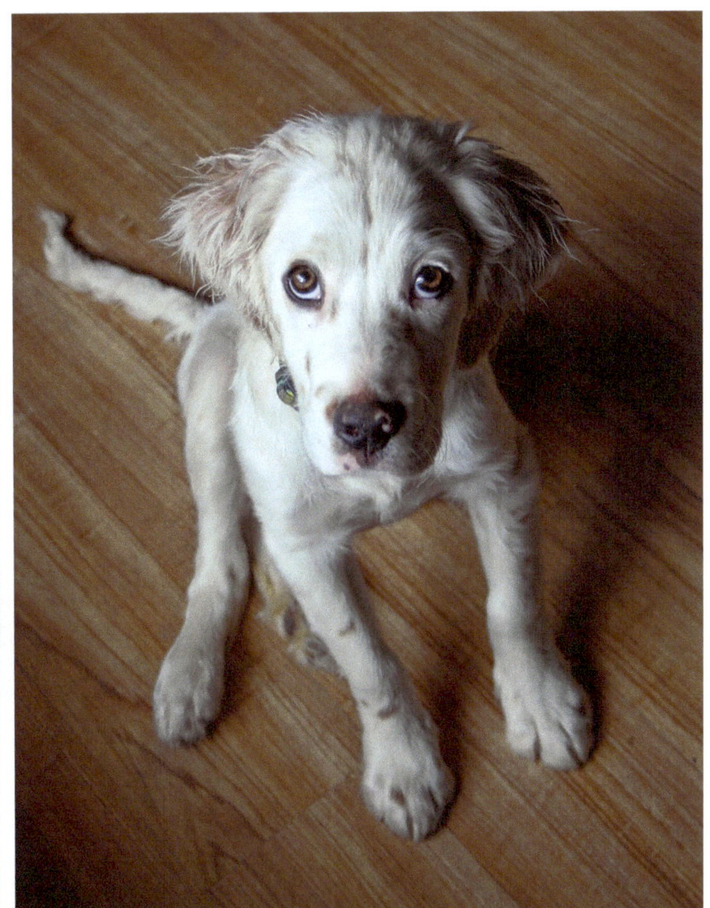
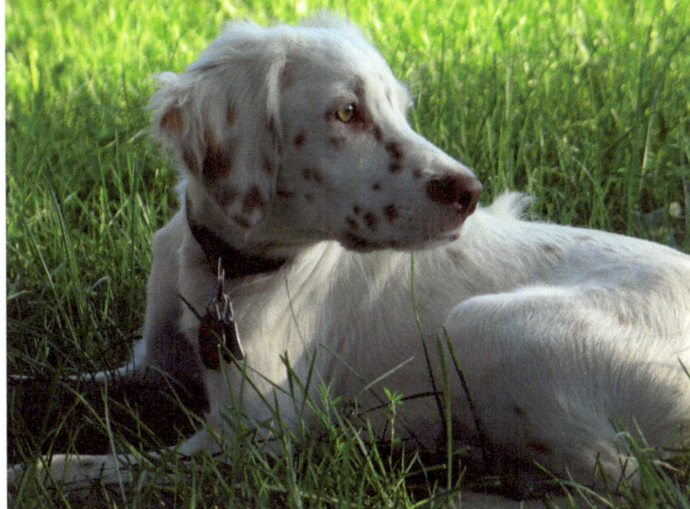

Bringing Home an Adult

English Setters live about 13 years, sometimes longer. Since they're bred to be active hunting dogs, older English Setters still have high energy levels, although not quite as much as a puppy's. The benefit to bringing home an older English Setter instead of a puppy is knowing exactly how wonderful they are as soon as you meet them. Most of them are house-trained, they've stopped teething, and their personalities are well-formed. An older Setter will usually be calmer but the hunting instincts are still there. Even a senior Setter will be happy to point out a bird.

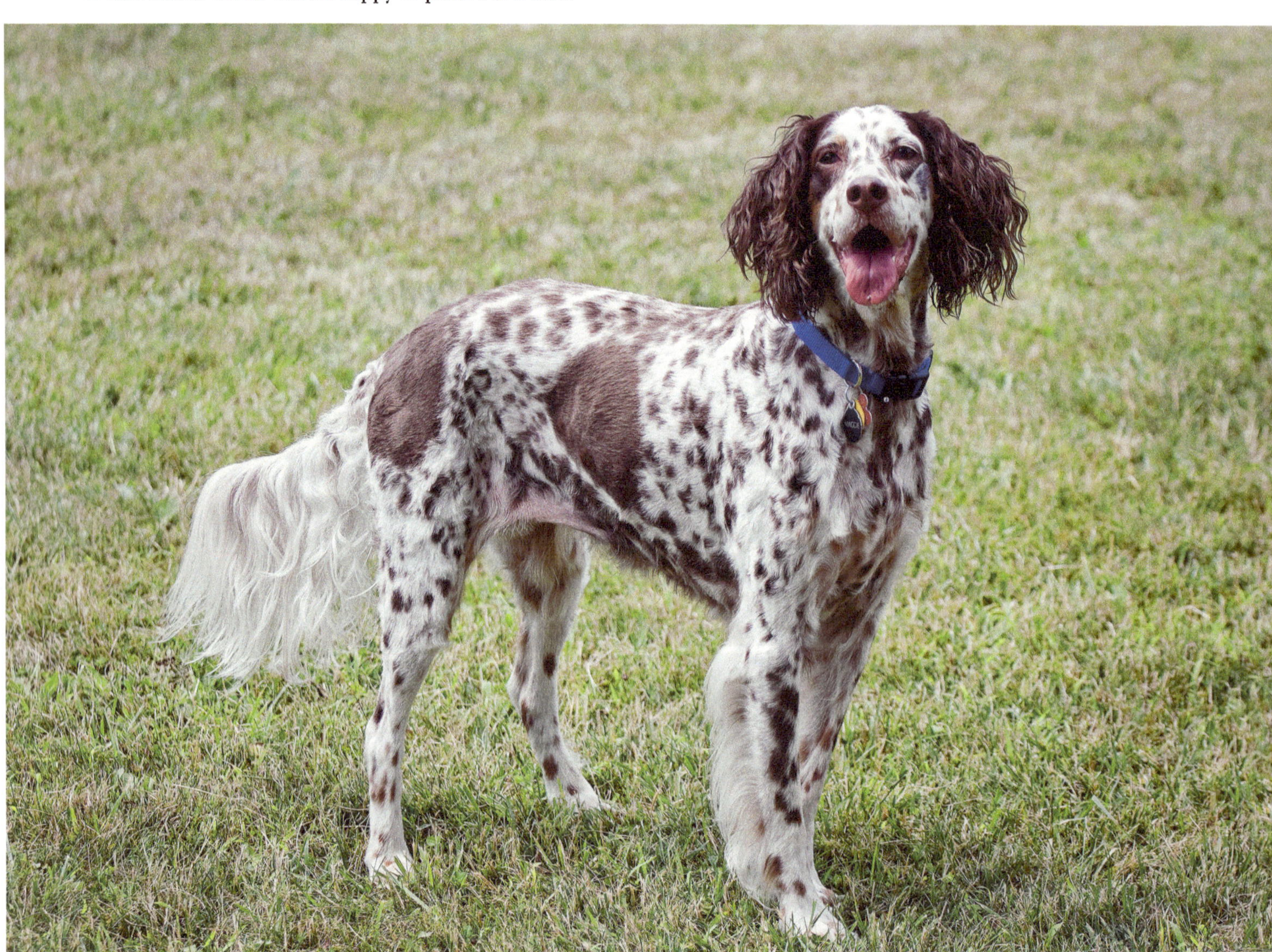

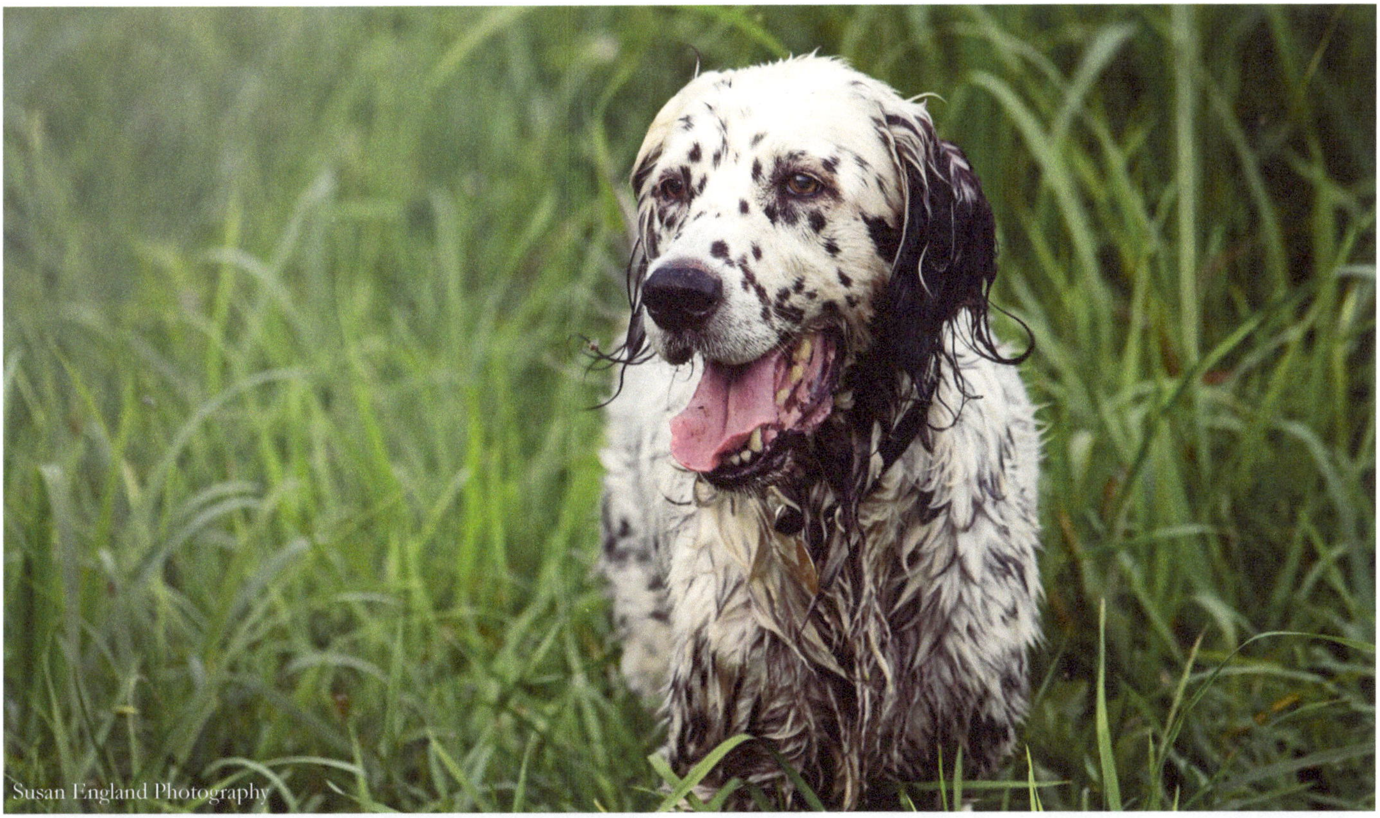

Susan England Photography

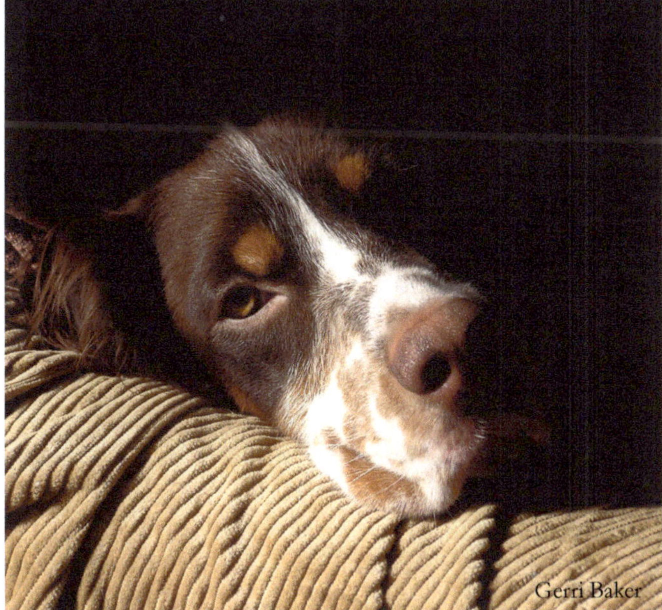

Gerri Baker

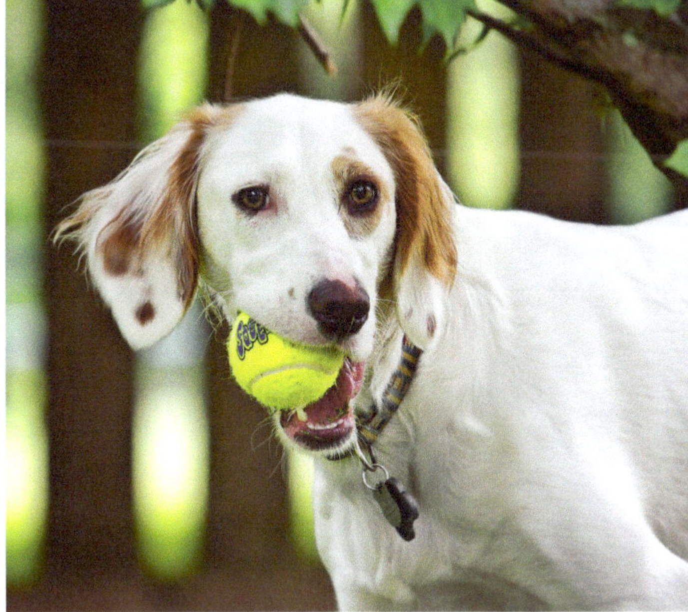

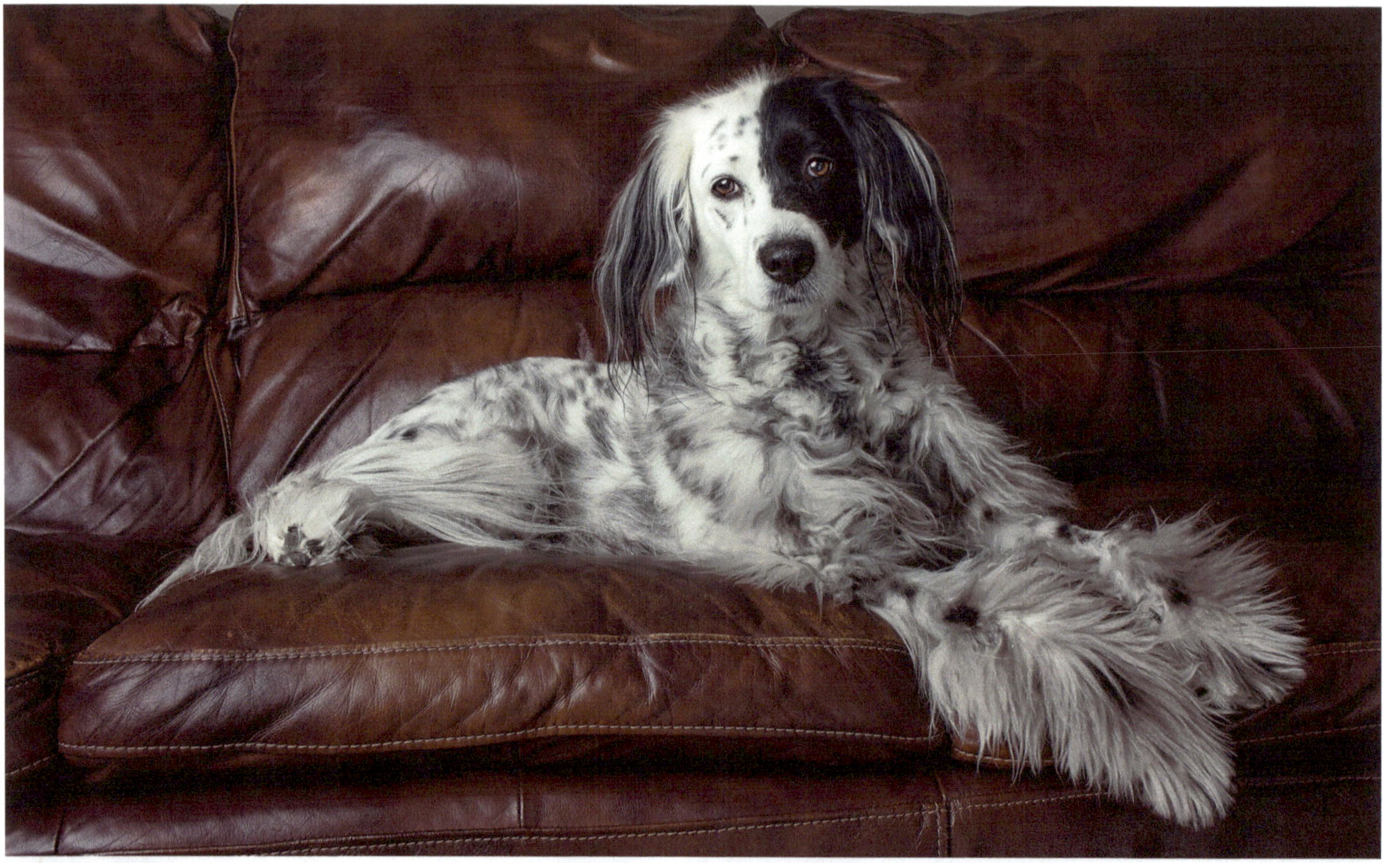

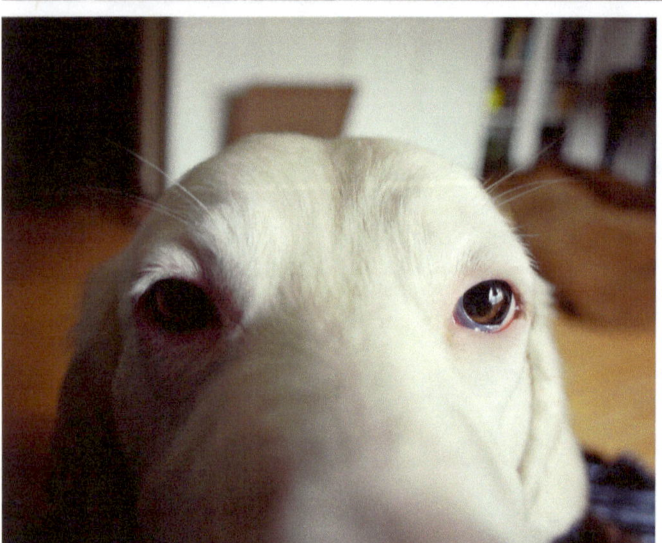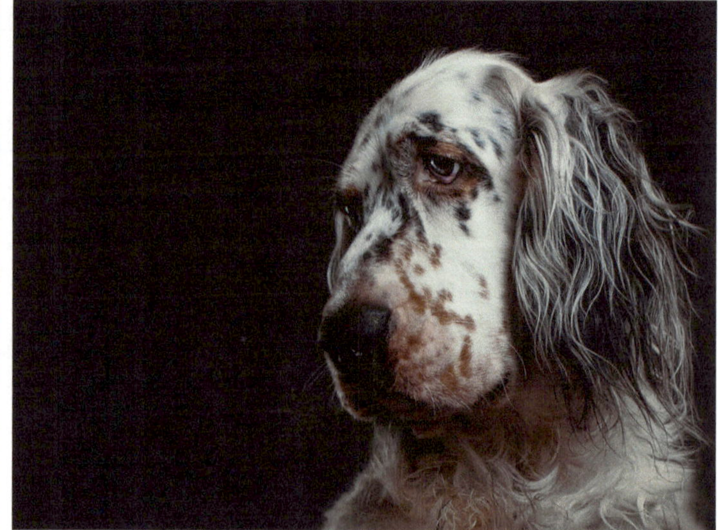

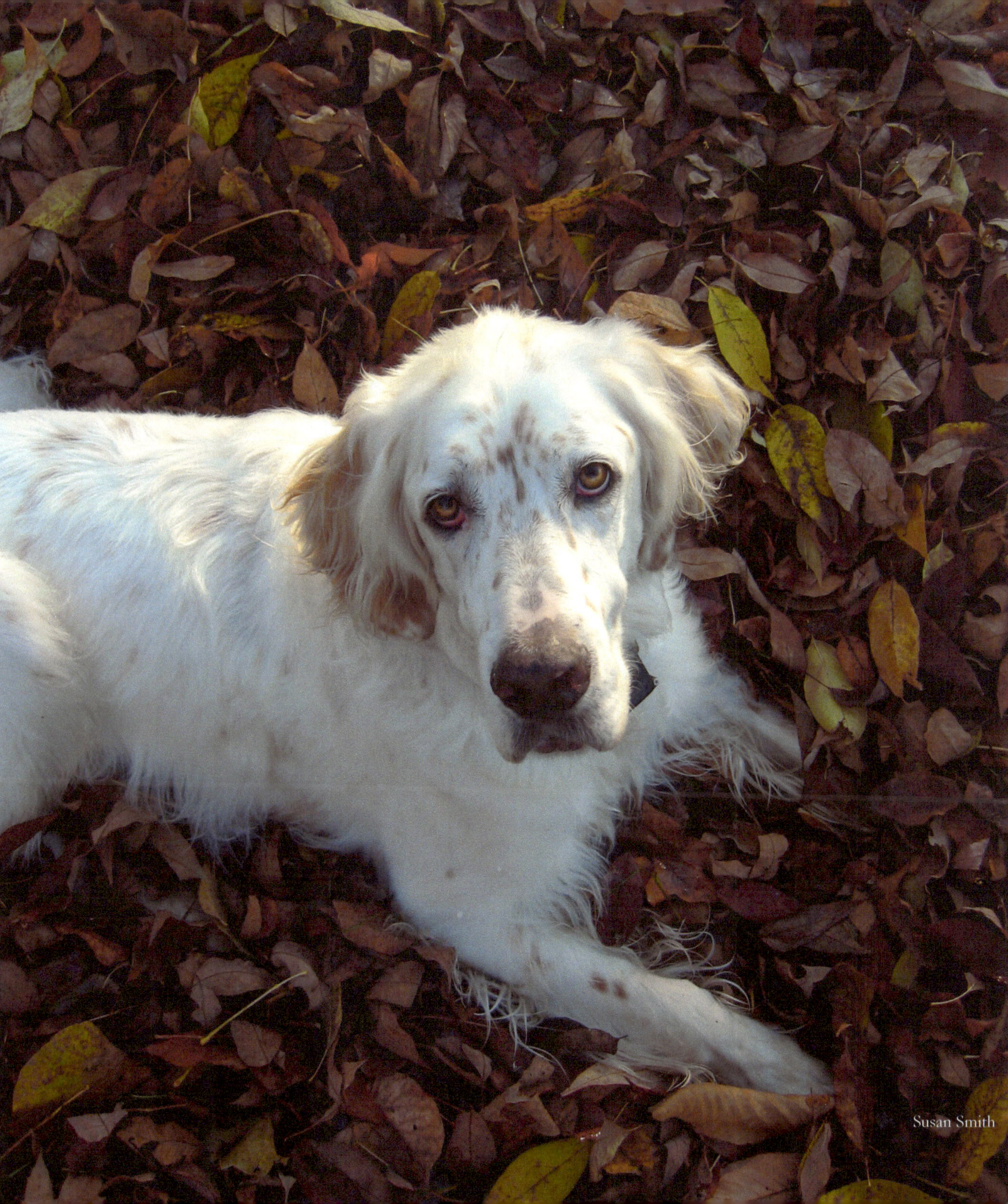
Susan Smith

English Setter Rescue

Dog rescues are non-profit organizations made up of individual volunteers who have opened their homes to dogs in order to provide them with a second chance. These "foster homes" work in much the same way as human foster homes. Dogs are paired with an appropriate foster family who provide a safe haven for the dogs to heal, regain confidence, and rebuild trust. A very important part of fostering is properly evaluating a foster dog for any health and behavioral issues. Understanding the dog's temperament is critical to match it with just the right family. Because those in rescue are so familiar with the trauma of abandonment, they are eager to place the dogs in the best homes. There are usually detailed adoption applications that have to be filled out first and then interviews with the foster families to make certain the dog will fit in well and have a permanent home.

There are breed-specific rescues which concentrate on a single type of dog. The advantages of breed-specific rescues are that they are very familiar with the characteristics of that breed and can usually provide potential adopters with more accurate information about the dogs in their care. There are many English Setter rescues in the United States as well as internationally.

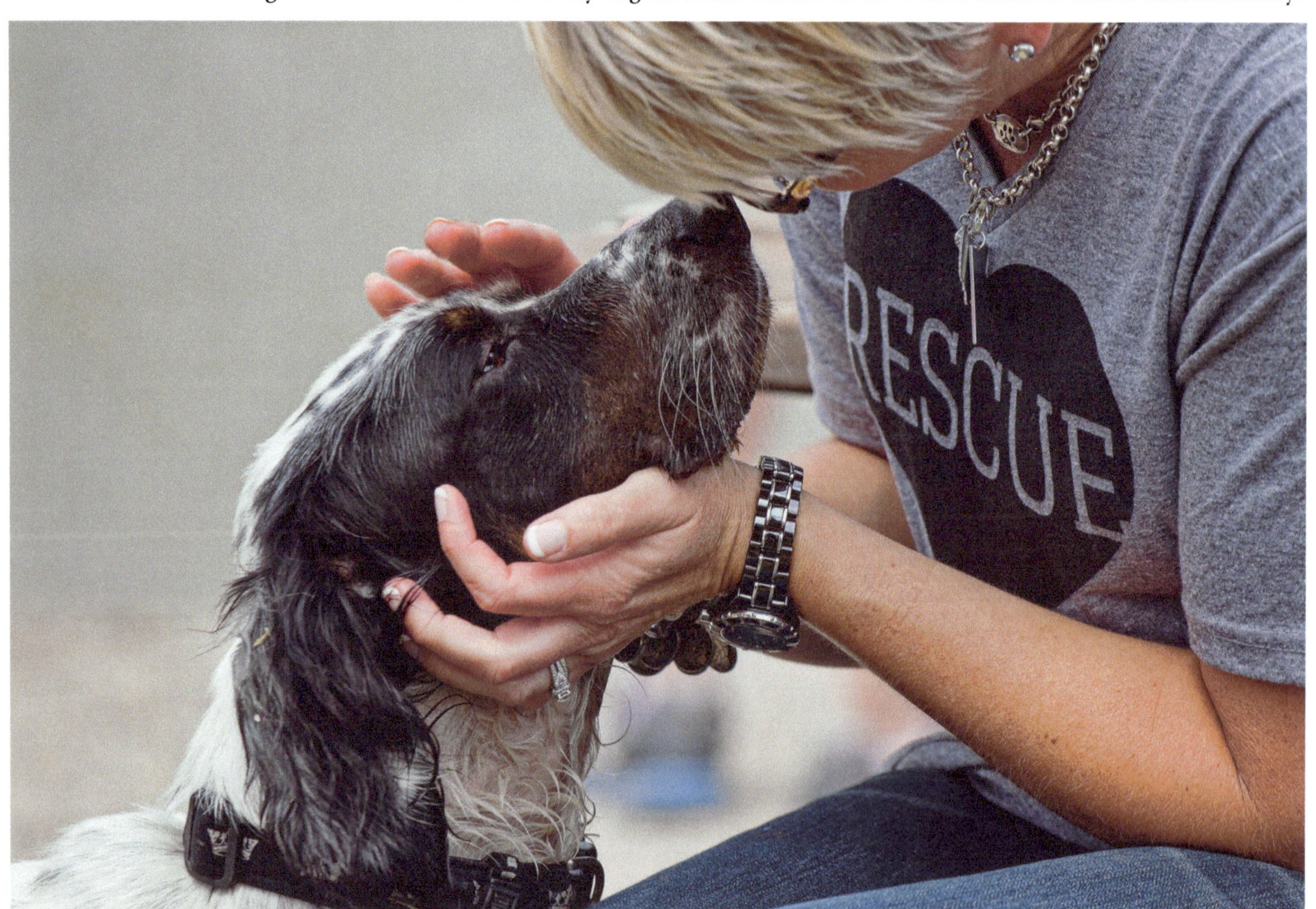

English Setters end up in rescue for a multitude of different reasons. Some of them are turned in by their owners. Others are transferred to rescue from shelters. By moving purebred dogs into a rescue for their breed, shelters can make room for other dogs. Some Setters were found as strays, their family's circumstances changed (move, new baby, divorce), the family didn't have enough time for the dog, the Setter wouldn't hunt, or was too energetic. Unfortunately, there are always English Setters of all types and ages waiting to be rescued.

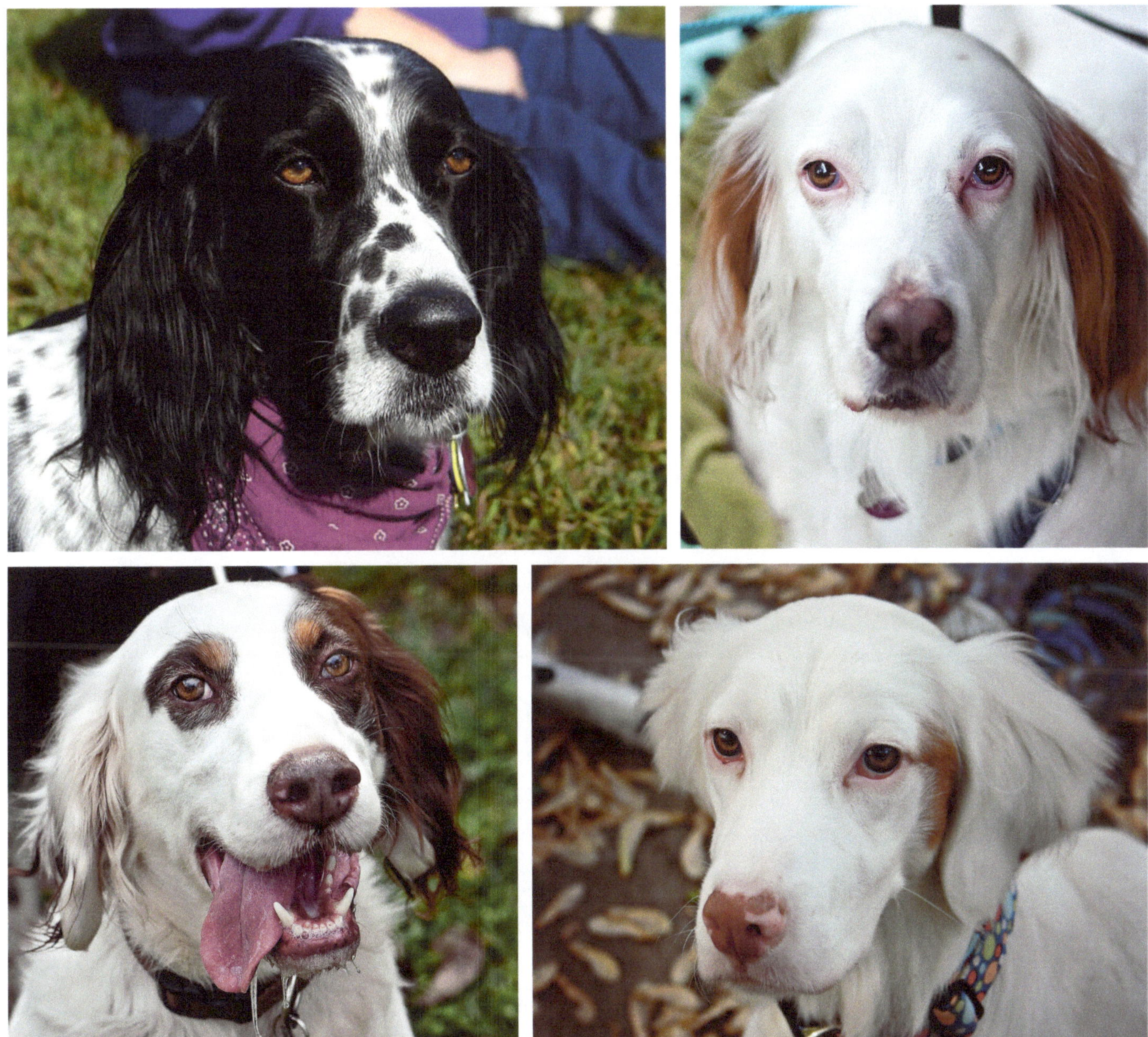

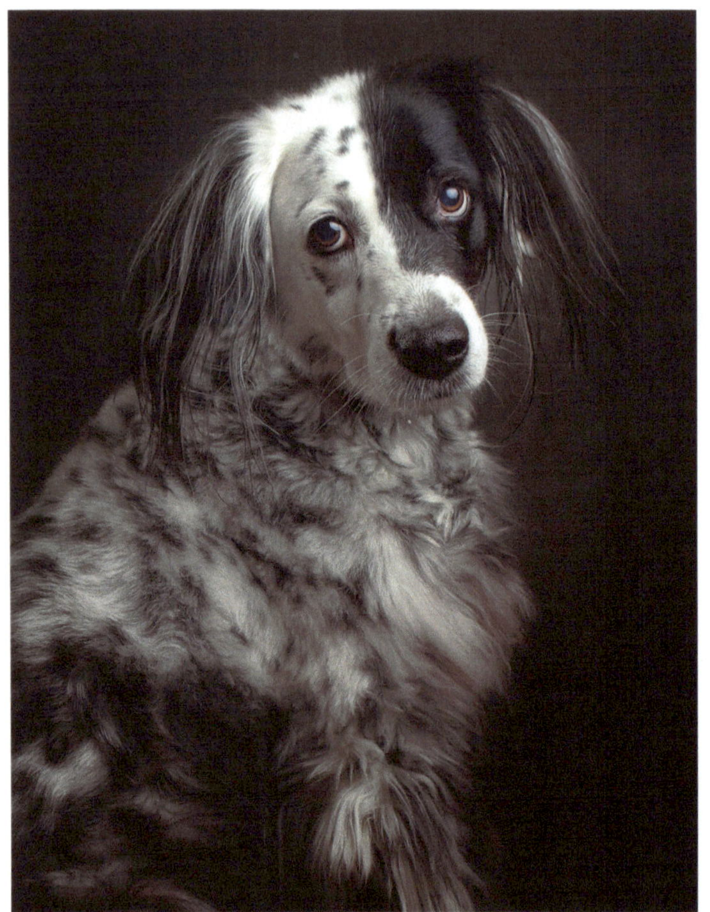

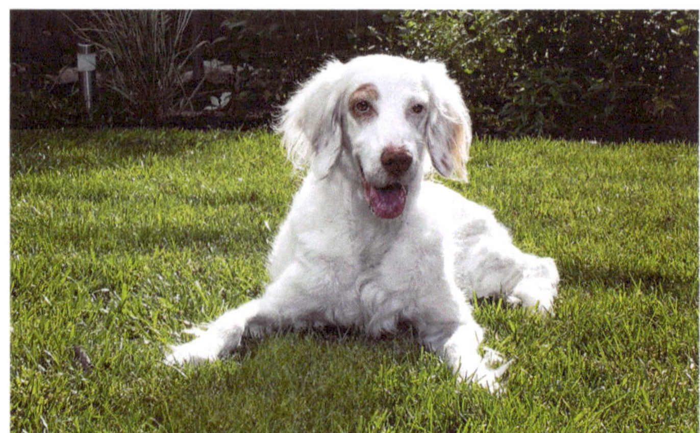

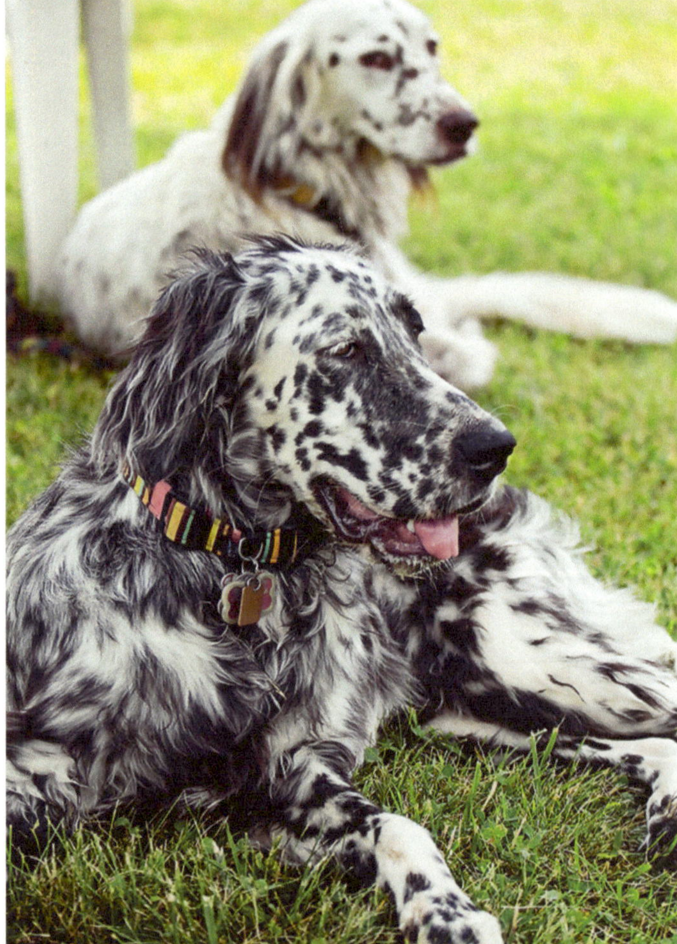

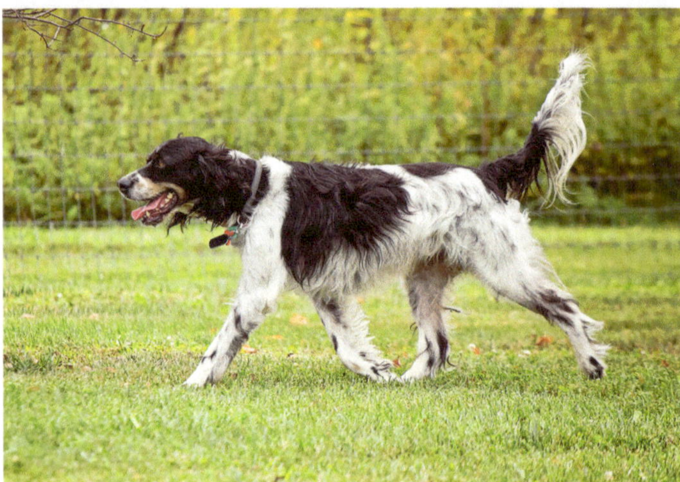

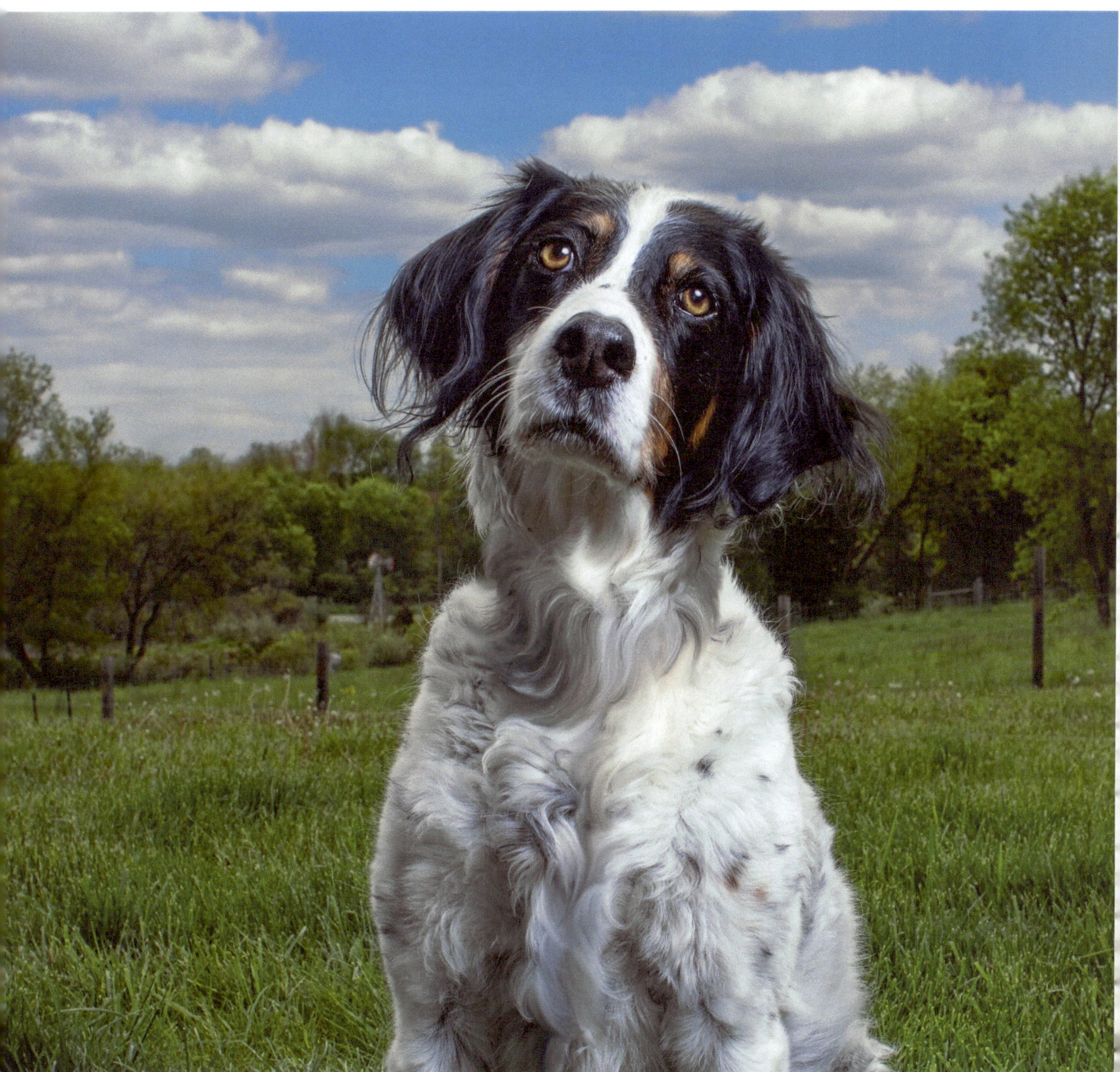

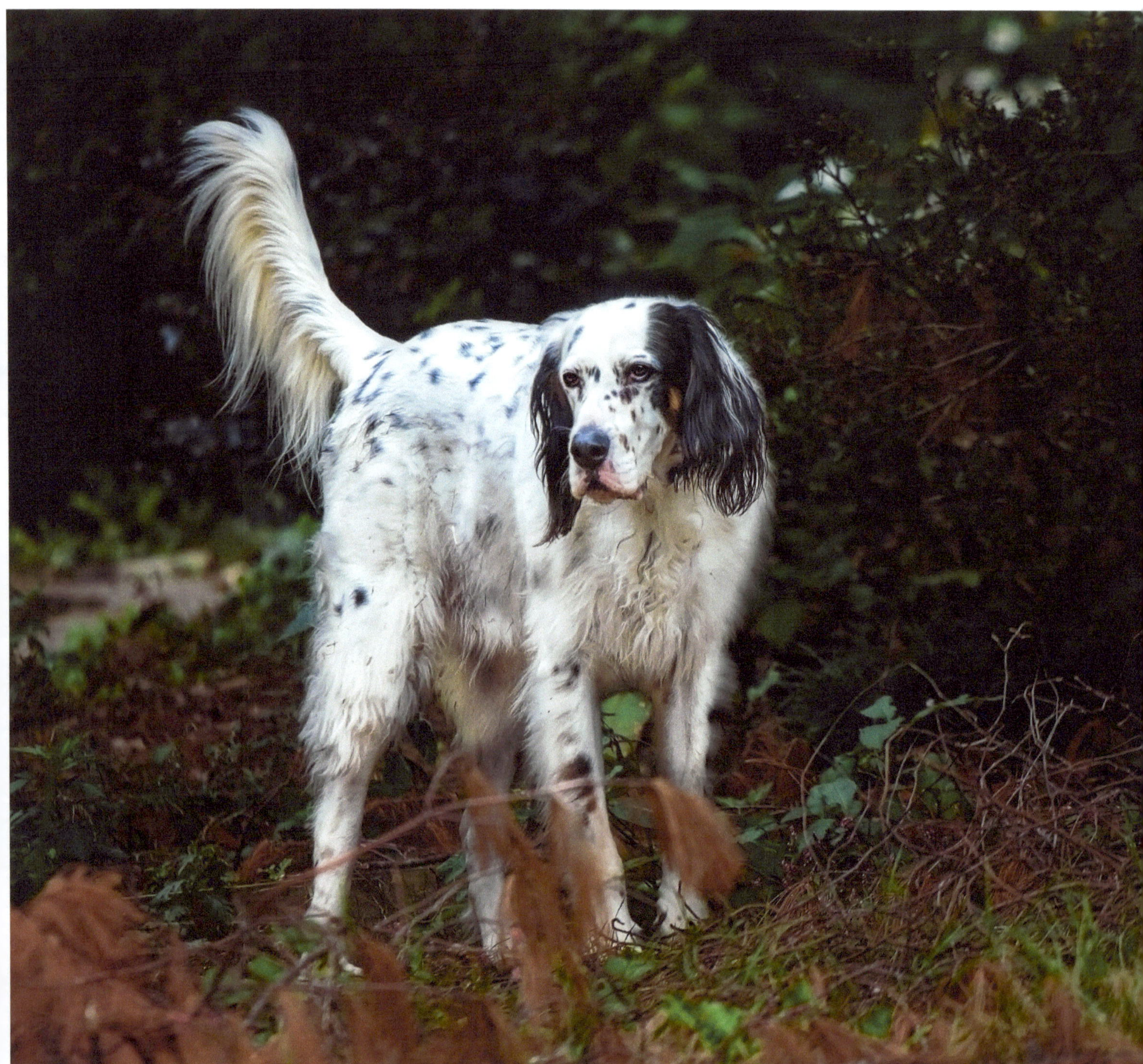

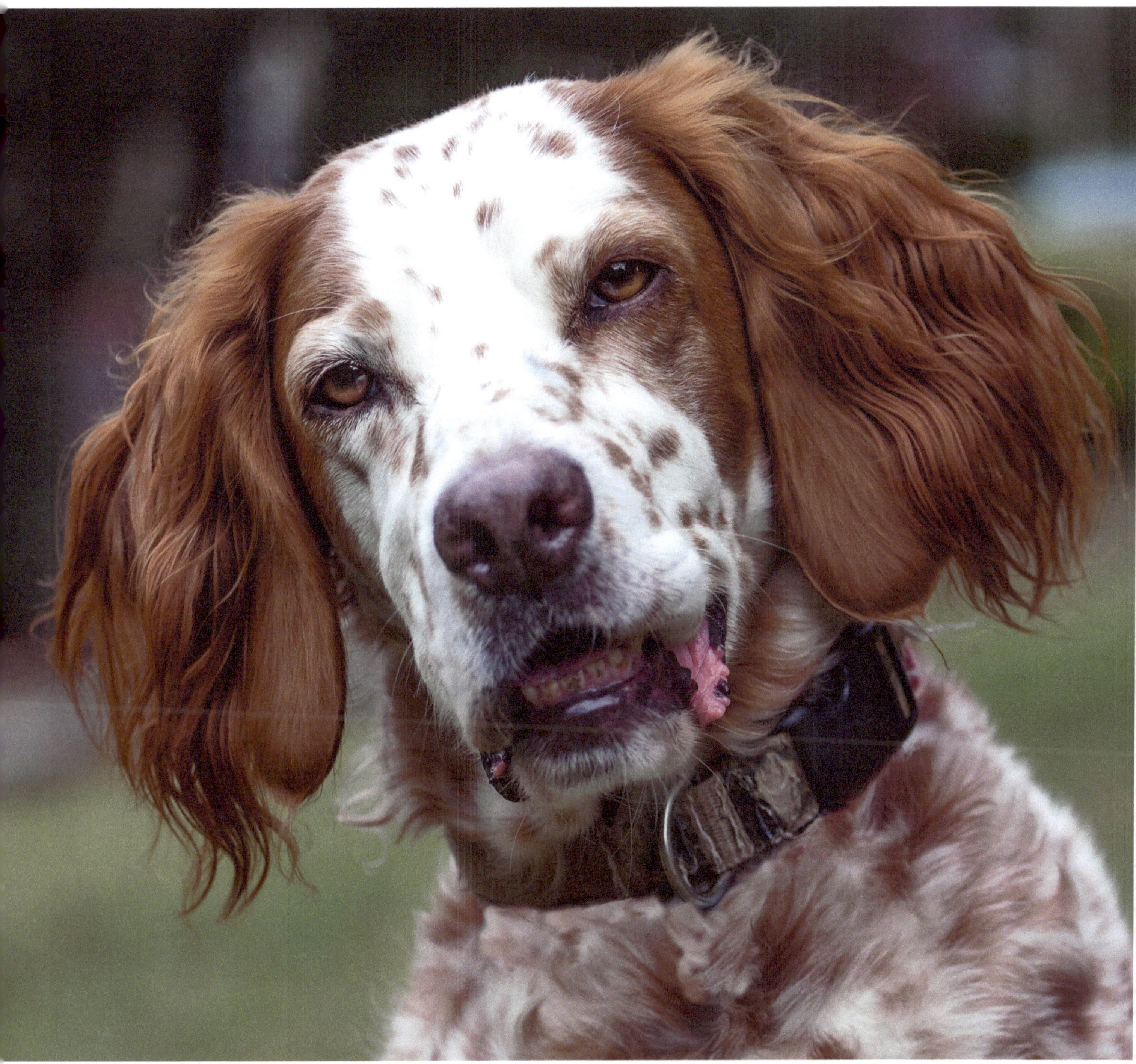

Acknowledgements

"Setterly Yours" (whose title is inspired by the signature block of my friend, Marcy Borelli) would not exist without the incredible support and passion of fellow Setter lovers world-wide. From Janice Harlow, my first Setter's foster mother who took my panicked phone calls and endless emails with patience and wisdom in those first two wild years, to the numerous Yahoo Group and Facebook friends who have opened their homes to me as I travelled cross-country with my Setters to photograph and meet yet more Setters. Carola and Jeff Clark, Bari Jackson, Greg and Pat Bonetti, Tim and Whitby Pratt, Crystal and Ross Johnson, Shannon Barry and Alex Rainboth, Paul and Elaine Tweedy, Diane and Kaycee Peterson, Holly Christensen and Stephen Krogulecki, and Dawn and Rob Mozgawa, thank you for welcoming a stranger, for not calling me crazy (openly), for answering my questions, and for listening and reading my stories.

And a big thank you to my wife who doesn't quite understand my fascination with this breed that demands so much of my undivided attention but continues to nod and smile when I talk about them endlessly and only sighs when I tell her I'm bringing home another one.

Although the majority of the photography in "Setterly Yours" is mine, I could not resist including the beautiful Setter photographs taken by my talented friends Andrew Lawlor (AndrewLawlorPhotography.com), Susan England (Susan England Photography), Holly Christensen, and Diane Peterson (Photos by DP). There is also a random sampling of English Setter photographers worldwide whose works I discovered on Flickr and who were all gracious enough to let me use their images in the first edition, republished here in the second edition. The section on the versatility of English Setters uses images provided by the owners of some amazing working dogs. All the dogs featured in the "Deaf Setters" section are actually deaf.

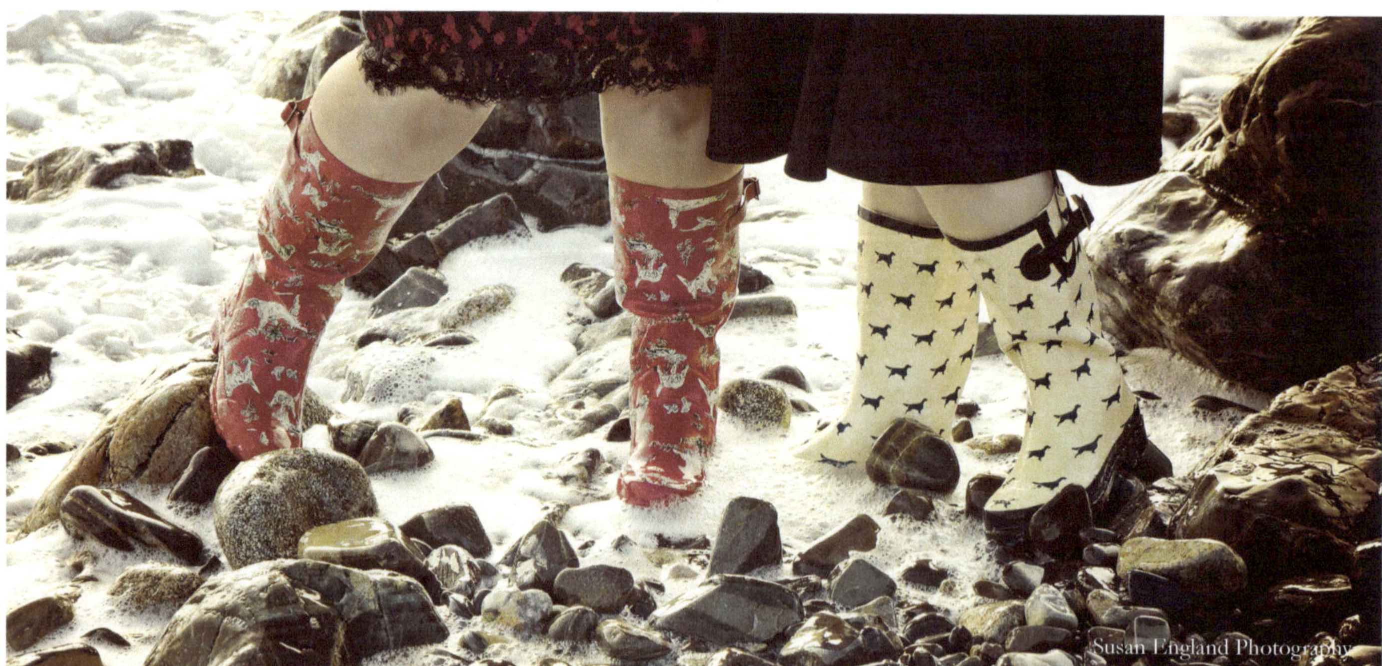

Susan England Photography

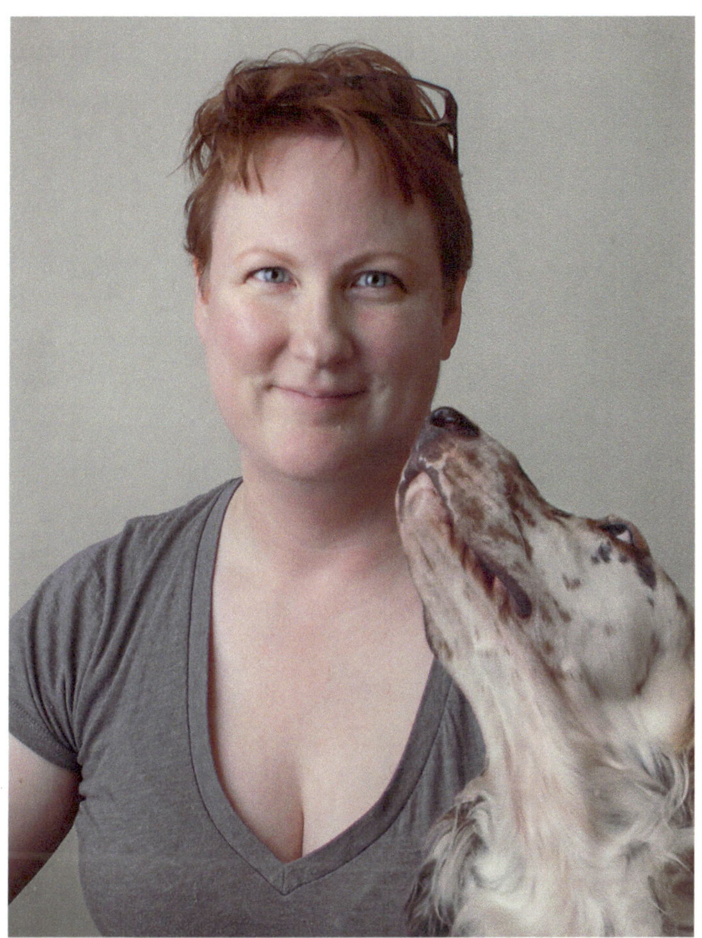

Danica Barreau lives in central Ohio with her menagerie and a very patient school teacher. Her childhood was spent in France and Germany and she moved to the US to attend her mother's alma mater, The Ohio State University. She dreamt of being a successful architect until the reality of math and physics and her love of color and fabrics drove her into the arms of Interior Design. That love affair lasted until the rent was due and then she took a corporate gig and has been working as a business analyst for a top telecom company for almost 20 years. In her spare time she manages to keep her home in some semblance of order while raising adorable English Setters, cooking fine meals, and pursuing her passion for photography. Her mother is a teacher and her father is a skilled gourmet cook which explains both her expanding waistline and her thoughtful use of the Oxford comma.

Danica is the owner and artist of Pouka Fine Art Pet Portraits (www.pouka.com), dedicated to fine art animal portraiture since 1998. She is a member of Professional Photographers of Ohio (PPO), Professional Photographers of America (PPA), and is pursuing her Certified Professional Photographer certification, as well as working on her Master of Photography and Master Artist degrees. Her dog photography (and her chili) has won a multitude of awards including a silver medal in the prestigious International Photographic Competition.

Danica has fostered a slew of English Setters for several rescues and owned a dog daycare for a few years. She does agility with her Setters and shares her experiences with living with deaf dogs to increase awareness and help other deaf dog owners. Danica wrote and published the first edition of "Setterly Yours" in 2009 and is currently brain-storming a children's book series featuring her youngest Setter, Finch.

Danica shoots a crop lens Canon 7D Mark II. Her preferred studio lens is a 24mm 2.8 although she also dallies with a 50mm 1.8, and 70-200mm 4-5.6 lenses. Her main OCF is a Flashpoint Rovelight 600 strobe, backed up by a Yongnuo 685 speedlight and a Canon 430ex II speedlight. Modifiers include a 60" octobox and a beauty dish.

To contact the author, email her at info@pouka.com or find her on Facebook under "Pouka Fine Art Pet Portraits".

Online Resources

DEAF SETTERS

Locations for BAER Testing
www.lsu.edu/deafness/baersite.htm

Information/Support for Deaf Dogs
www.deafdogs.org
www.deafdogsrock.com
FB: Deaf Setter Mamas

ENGLISH SETTER RESCUE

501c3 registered English Setter Rescues in the United States
Another Chance for English Setter: www.englishsetterrescue.org
Our English Setter Rescue: www.oesr.org
Above and Beyond English Setter Rescue: www.esrescue.org
Southwest English Setter Rescue: www.swesr.org
A Better English Setter Rescue: www.abetteresetter.org

English Setter Rescue in the UK
The English Setter Rescue Association: www.englishsetterrescue.co.uk

ENGLISH SETTER BREED INFORMATION

American Kennel Club: www.akc.org/breeds/english_setter
The Ryman-Type Hunting English Setter: www.rymansetters.com
The Old Hemlock Foundation: www.oldhemlock.org

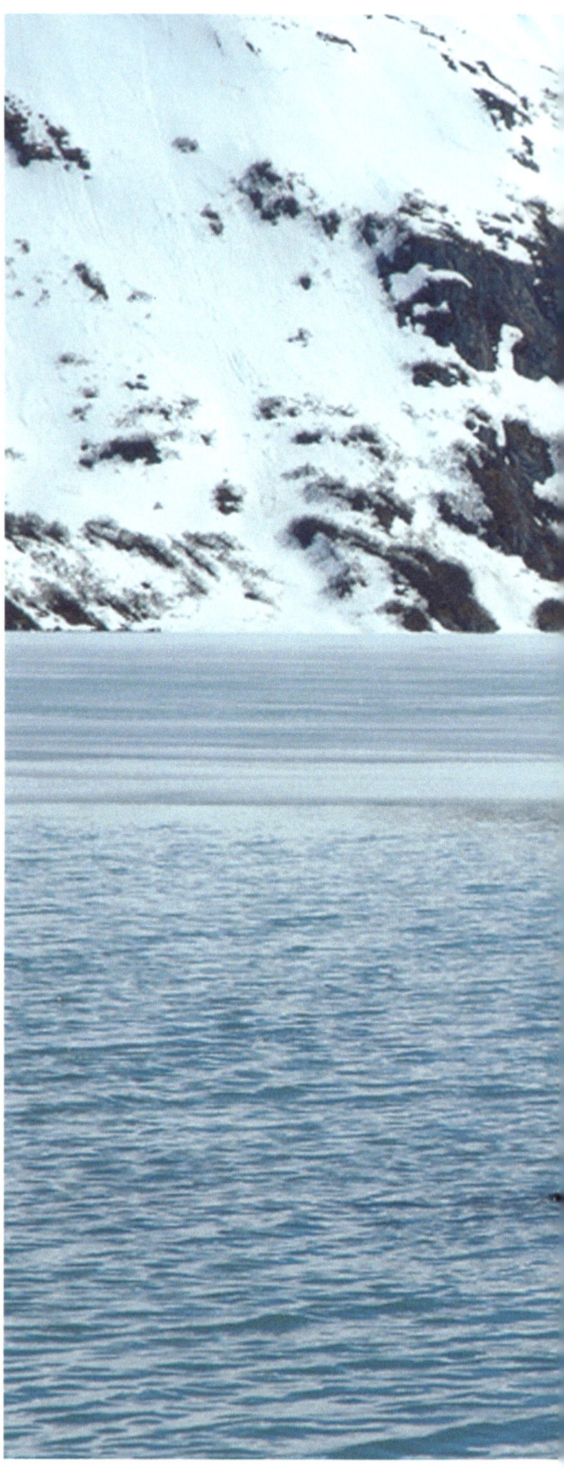

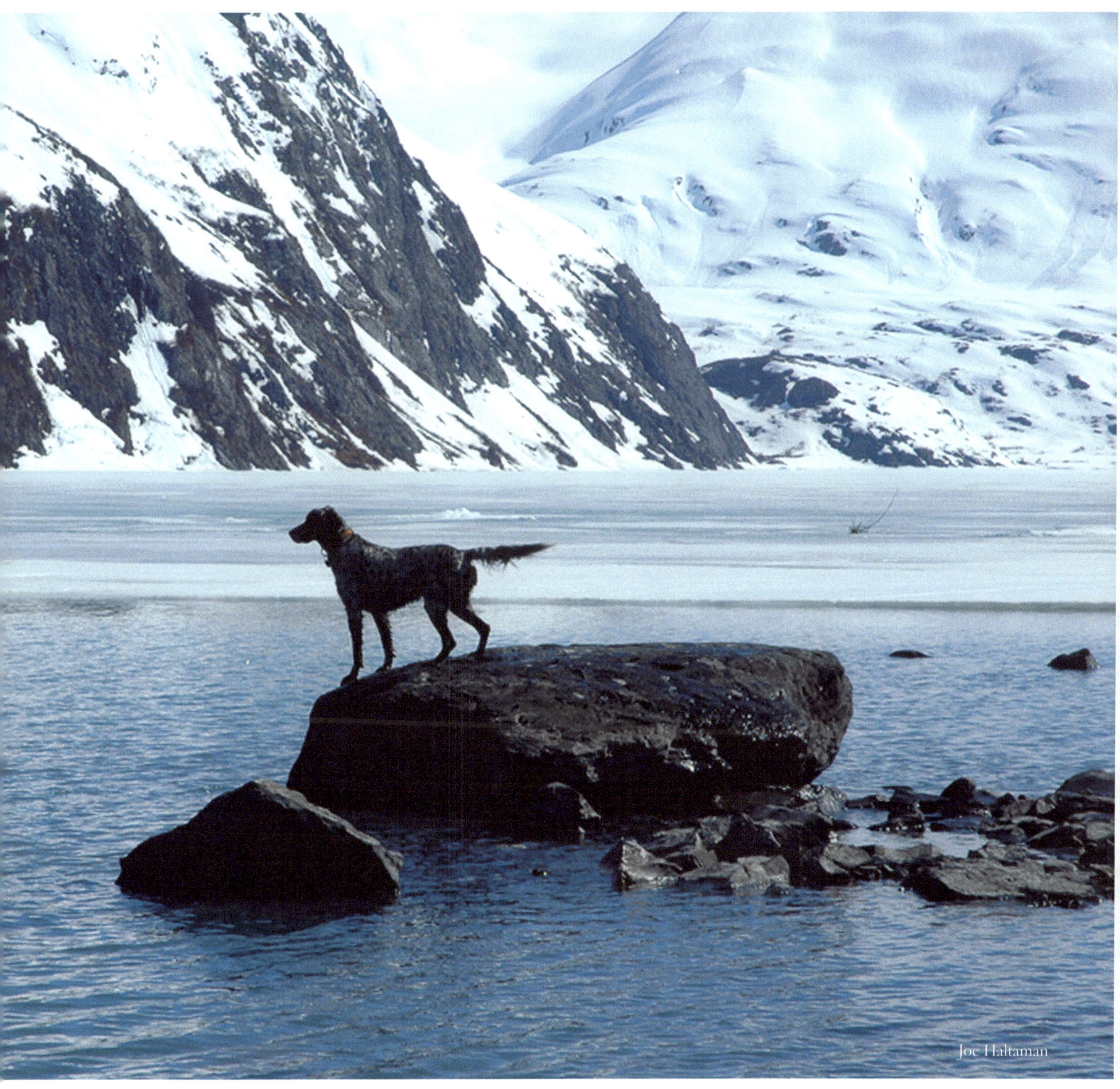
Joe Haltaman

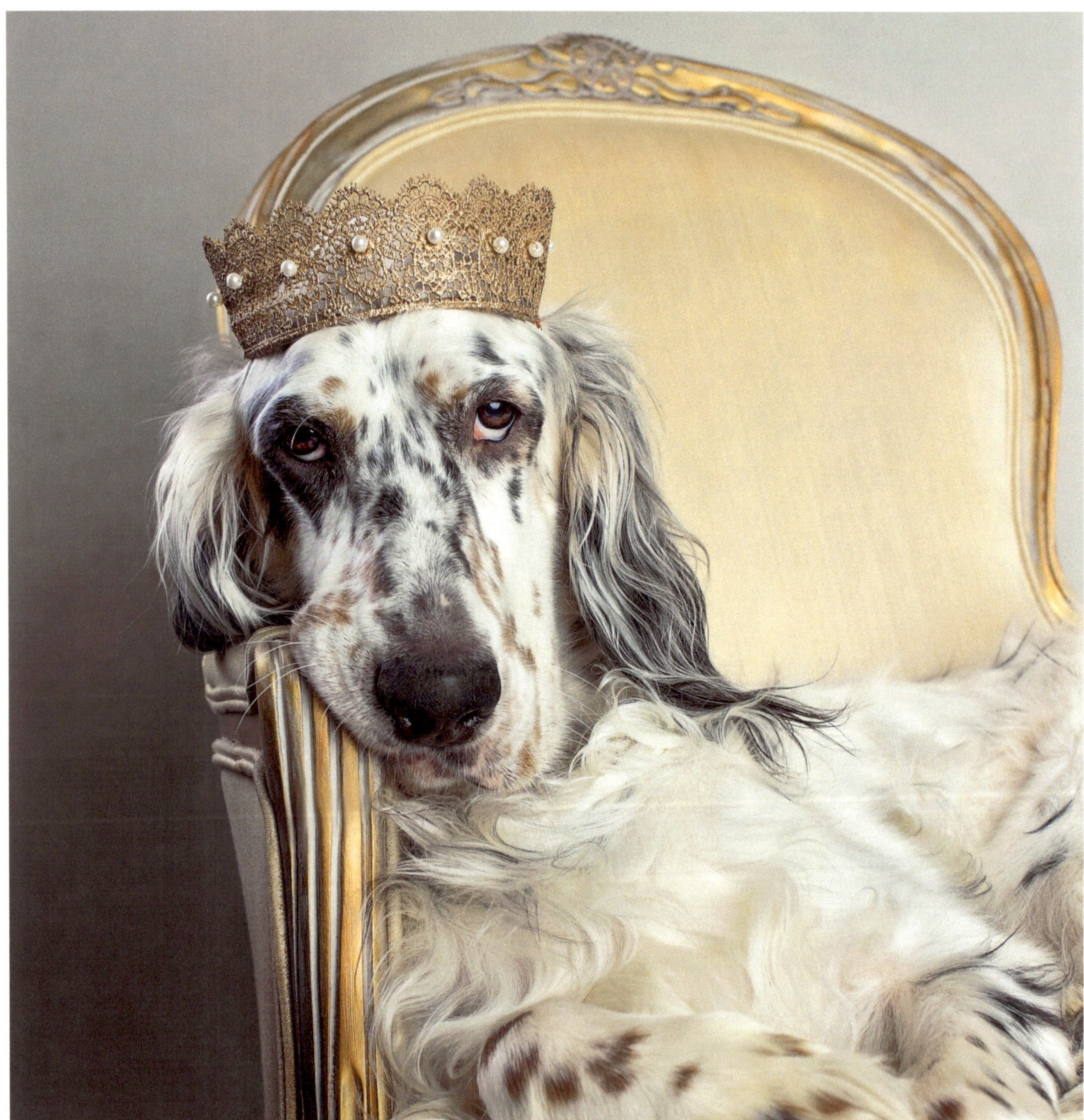

LETTER ON PUPPY SOCIALIZATION by Dr. R.K. Anderson, DVM, Diplomat American College of Veterinary Preventive Medicine and Diplomat American College of Veterinary Behaviorists.

GENETICS AND INHERITANCE OF CANINE DEAFNESS by Dr. George M. Strain, Louisiana State University Comparative Biomedical Sciences, School of Veterinary Medicine, Baton Rouge, Louisiana 70803

THE ESSENCE OF SETTERS: AN IN-DEPTH STUDY OF THE FOUR SETTERS by Marsha Hall Brown. Doral Publishing, 2002.

THE SETTER by Lynn Hamilton and Edward Laverack. Lynn Hamilton, 1999.

ENGLISH SETTERS by Beverly Pisano. TFH Publications, 1997.

THE HISTORY OF ENGLISH SETTER SHOWDOGS IN AMERICA by Craig S. Sparkes. Doral Publishing, 2003.

A GENTLEMAN'S SHOOTING DOG: THE EVOLUTION OF THE LEGENDARY RYMAN SETTER by John D. Taylor. Bonasa Press, 2004.

THE NEW COMPLETE ENGLISH SETTER by Davis H. Tuck. Howell Book House, Inc., 1981.

ABOUT ACES - retrieved May 16, 2009 from: http://www.englishsetterrescue.org.

DEAFNESS IN DOGS - retrieved May 21, 2009 from: http://www.deafdogs.org/faq.

SURVEY OF DEAF ENGLISH SETTER OWNERS by Danica Barreau. Responses to surveys collected online on February 19, 2015.